ISBN 978-1-332-01828-4
PIBN 10269590

THE "TA-NEHESU": THE COUNTRY OF THE BLACKS.

Frontispiece.

IN THE TORRID SUDAN

BY H. LINCOLN TANGYE, F.R.G.S.
AUTHOR OF 'IN NEW SOUTH AFRICA'

WITH MAPS AND ILLUSTRATIONS

BOSTON
RICHARD G. BADGER
THE GORHAM PRESS
1910

PRINTED IN GREAT BRITAIN

TO

ANNIE GILZEAN TANGYE

PREFACE

BEYOND the recollection of the Dervish revolt, the death of Gordon, and Kitchener's triumph, the name Sudan conveys but little impression to many who have not the opportunity of personally visiting the regions included under that name.

While the bibliography of the country is considerable, with little exception it was to a great extent merely exploratory and speculative until Count Gleichen put on record an immense amount of the detailed observations of various experts, and, more recently, Dr. Wallis Budge, with his great fund of accumulated knowledge and personal research, compiled two large historical volumes of absorbing interest. The labours of the Wellcome Research Laboratories have also added considerably to scientific information as to the conditions of the country and people, and Sir Harry Johnston has contributed important studies. I have referred freely to these various works, and have had the opportunity of converse with various authorities resident in the country.

The aim of the following pages is to show the Sudan, or some portions of it, as it appears to the present-day observer, to the student of mankind and the lover of Nature, living and still; to describe the amenities of sport and travel in widely separated districts amongst varied peoples, one of which was new in submission to the white man; with a concise review of sociological conditions and of a history which is more or less unknown to the multitude.

H. LINCOLN TANGYE.

MAXSTOKE CASTLE,
WARWICKSHIRE.

CONTENTS

LIST OF ILLUSTRATIONS

IN THE TORRID SUDAN

CHAPTER I

INTRODUCTORY

WELL on to two decades ago it was my fortune, after much wandering in "New South Africa"—or what then was the "newest" South Africa—to write on the manifold problems which at that time confronted the student and politician there, and to hazard a conjecture as to their ultimate solution which, sooner than even the most sanguine, and more satisfactorily than the most optimistic could have possibly ventured to hope for, has in this year come to pass.

The uniting of the "States of South Africa" has become an accomplished fact. The mutual respect caused by the demonstration to each combatant of the sterling qualities of the other was born during a period of three years' warfare which put to the test every attribute of manhood on either side, and formed the basis for a junction of interests. But more than this: with the removal of irreconcilable and unstatesmanlike factors—both Boer and British

—a condition of harmony and peace has been evolved which promises well for the future of a confederation which has already given evidences that it is proud of its loyalty to the Empire of which it now forms no mean a portion.

At the time when gloom and uncertainty reigned in South Africa, the intermediate regions were peopled by hordes but incompletely brought under the influence of civilization, while chaos and barbarism were supreme in the far north beyond the Great Lakes.

The "Ta-Nehesu," the "Sudan," the "Country of the Blacks," as it has been known from time immemorial, was, for not by any means the first time in its history, in the throes of a desperate revolt against advancing civilization, decimating and almost destroying itself in the process.

When that civilization is in itself half barbaric, when religious sentiment comes to the aid of resentment, and the crude, selfish instincts of primitive man are let loose, then are developed the moral conditions essential as a foundation for reactionary success.

All these conditions existed when the Mahdi arose and headed the Arab revolt. The civilization of the Egyptian Government was for the most part veneer and covered the vilest abuses; men's minds became receptive of extraordinary ideas and beliefs, to a great extent adapted to their political aims, and the ferocity of unhampered savagedom supplied the last factor.

The true civilization came too late on the scene. Its spasmodic efforts had been stemmed by the dead-weight of vested interests in Cairo and Khartoum ; Great Britain would not move, being jealously watched by the Powers and fearful of the magnitude of the task as compared with the apparent ultimate gain ; Gordon had died after being sent to Khartoum to retire the alien civilians and garrisons ; and not until dreadful developments had ensued was it thoroughly realized that the alternatives had been civilization or virulent barbarism, and that barbarism triumphantly menaced a continent.

When a people's nerves get out of joint, the very violence of the cataclysm leads to a cure through sheer self-exhaustion. This was the case in the great revolution of France, when, though so many innocent suffered, the bad also turned upon bad to the community's purification. So also in the Dervish Sudan, more or less honest ideals deteriorated on achievement of victory, or the need of the mask was lost sight of; Arab fell upon Arab while the slow insistence of an inexorable wave gathered strength in the north. Murder and extermination, vice and corruption, did their work, and while the warlike qualities of the people, their faith in the Khalifa as a soldier, and their hatred of the Christian, sufficed to give cohesion to many, their numbers were not as before, neither was the vigour of their fanaticism so overwhelming nor the power of resistance so great.

So the cloud of misrule was dispersed; on every artery, at the seat of each nerve, came the grasp of the white man, who rules for his people and not for himself, and whose endeavours are devoted to making his people peaceful, contented, prosperous, developing them materially and mentally.

How different the conditions in the Sudan to those in most parts of South Africa! Yet they have to some extent their parallel. Few would say that the Sudan is a territory which a white man, barring the misanthrope, would wish to make the home of his lifetime. But the same might be urged of the Karroo, which is not obviously interesting. The most important factor is the climate, for few places are free from malaria, and there is not generally the range of altitude which is a boon to South Africa.

Moreover, the water-supply is aggravating in its partiality and the extremes of its fluctuations, being in quantity either too much or too little, and the water obtainable in useful quarters is mostly bespoken for Egypt. In time this will be regulated by the undertaking of works which will distribute the water which now goes to waste in morasses.

The direction of effort in the Sudan will lie as much in the way of developing the country's resources by its inhabitants for its inhabitants as by Europeans for Europeans; but no mean element in this endeavour lies in the need of education of the native to overcome indolence, and to discard ancient and inefficient methods and applianecs.

Where the European comes in is, of course, in constructive enterprises, or undertakings involving large tracts of ground and requiring considerable capital, and it is in these directions mainly that occupation for young Europe will open.

Certainly the contemplated supply of water to the Ghezireh from the Blue Nile will provide opportunity for cotton-growing on a suitable scale, though the quality of the product, as at present placed on the market, requires considerable improvement. Some classes of rubber-producing trees are native to the Bahr-el-Ghazal, and the fitness of its conditions for the varieties generally favoured is now being tested.

Still, the education of the natives proceeds apace; while the Greeks—merchants, speculators and contractors—are omnipresent and make the country their home, so that the field for Europeans proper will more or less follow the lines of that of Egypt, though under more trying conditions.

Year by year, under the fostering care of the British Mudirs, production increases and methods improve, and in due course—though "hustle" is unknown in the Sudan—it will take rank as a highly important source of supply.

It has often been charged as a shortcoming of Great Britain that her traders insufficiently study their markets, so can it be wondered at that the careless Sudani, who for thousands of years have been content with primitive appliances and insouciant inexactness, find difficulty in appreciating the demand for a cotton free from dust and extraneous particles ?

The Arab character cannot be compared with that of the indigenous races. Tenacious, intelligent, commercial, and experienced, as are the more developed classes and the Arabs of purer blood, none are more eminently capable of appreciating immediate advantage, notwithstanding the custom and prejudice which are so antagonistic to progress. Whatever may be the Arab's vices and shortcomings, however hardened and callous where the sufferings of others are concerned, he has a power of initiative, an impelling and organizing force which takes him much farther than the mere production of hardly sufficient to live on, as is the case with so many of the negroids.

History has given examples of great powers of organization, and of an influence in which, whether exercised for good or for evil, intellect has taken chief place. The subconscious momentum of a ruling and dominant race, inherited from Asiatic forefathers, has carried them onward, and from the east to the west and far to the south they have conquered and spread. They have the imaginative power which permits of a highly developed religious system, a docility to its teaching and an extravagance in its translation born partly of elementary fanaticism, and partly of an unshakable belief in the safety of their own eternal future, involving a general reliance on unadulterated selfishness.

What if these peoples had not been the subjects of failings as great as their inherent powers? What if principles of humanity, progress, and development, had gained sway in place of the cramping influences of a religion, or perhaps, to be strictly just, the interpretation of it, which warps while it yet binds together, permits a fatalism which enervates in one direction while it gives force in another, and an egotism which runs riot between an extreme of literal observance of religious formulæ on one hand and the slavery and destruction of fellow-man for selfish ends on the other? Had enlightened ideals found a favourable ground on the basis of strength and of intellect, a rule of great power over vast areas of Africa would have been created, almost unassailable in its position.

It is the "kismet" on the part of the vast majority, the lack of inherent as distinguished from prescribed morality on the part of vast numbers, the inappreciation of the value of time, and, except under extraordinary stimulus, the lack of cohesion, which limit the expansive power of this remarkable race.

The people of the Sudan, mixed in blood as many are, nevertheless are sharply divided into three classes—the Arabs or pseudo-Arabs of the north (for these show many divergencies from the original Asiatic type); the negroids of the south, many of whom were doubtless pushed up-river by the invading ancient Egyptians and subsequent Arab irruptions; and certain tribes, including the

Kordofan Nubas and the Barabras, who are thought to be the descendants of the original opponents of the ancients. That the negroid survives after centuries of ravage, spoliation, and intertribal warfare, speaks volumes for his persistence in living; his physique under trying climatic conditions is a proof of his vitality, for the fever-stricken swamps of the Bahr-el-Ghazal appear less destructive of stature and strength than the factories of Europe.

Divided into a vast number of tribes, incohesive, fickle in their alliances except under extraordinary stimulus, the varied inhabitants of the Sudan yet exhibit cosmical characteristics, for their differing occupations render them considerably interdependent.

Particular tribes, such as those of Darfur and the nomads of the Bayuda desert, specialize in camel-breeding, the latter being famous for the swift hagin; the Baggara are noted for their cattle and horses; the Dongolese for their dates; salt is produced in many localities, and iron, less important in these days of importation, is smelted by even such savage tribes as the Jur and Bongo, for the purpose of being manufactured into spear-heads and hippo harpoons, considerable skill being shown.

Pacification and instruction are proceeding surely and with remarkable success. Sporadic outbursts, mainly fanatical or purely savage, occasionally occur, and in the less accessible districts it is sometimes necessary to demonstrate the warlike qualities of the "friends of peace," whose motives are to a great extent incomprehensible to the native mind. One excellent soldier of the 10th Sudanese, a late Dervish opponent, speaking of an expedition with the British into a little-known country, stated that he could not understand the English—they did not seem to *want* to come to blows, although when they did they were keen enough; when *he* went among an alien people, all he longed for was to have a fine *fight*.

It cannot be denied, however, that underneath an appearance of calmness lie smouldering fires. The ambitions of the slave traders cannot easily be eradicated; the smart caused by the suppression of that most lucrative of occupations, and the consequent interference with the Arab social fabric, still irritates; the inherent detestation of an infidel rule, however tolerant, and echoes of the Nationalist movement in Egypt, and indeed of events in Asia, combine to render "Fire and Sword in the Sudan" once again eminently possible, though the "iron horse" yearly renders revolutionary success less attainable.

A magnificent work lies before the rulers of the Sudan, a great field for the exercise of the finest attributes of an imperial race. Much has been accomplished, with an earnestness and devotion on the part of officials which must command the admiration of all who have eyes to see; the clouds of chaos and barbarism are being gradually dispersed, and the foundations have been laid of a State which, diversities and divergencies notwithstanding, will, under European guidance, assert its right to a respected and useful place among the countries of the earth.

CHAPTER II

PAST AGES OF CONQUEST

To enter a country without knowing something of its history is to rob the experience of half its usefulness and pleasure. Those who are ignorant of it see but half what may be seen, and that which does come before them is imperfectly appreciated. This must be my excuse for inflicting the following rough and imperfect summary of the history of many thousand years as it is recounted by the most eminent authorities.

The history of the Anglo-Egyptian Sudan is so intimately associated with its physical characteristics and geographical position that a foreword of description is essential to a proper understanding.

As it is known now it is almost entirely an inland country, bounded on the north by Egypt alone, against which it imposes formidable defences of desert by land, and boulder-strewn rapids by river.

On the east its character is more varied, possessing a frontage on the Red Sea, of inestimable importance to a country otherwise surrounded by various states. Following the eastern frontier southward, the Italian colony of Erithrea and the great empire of Abyssinia, on the water-supply from whose hills Egypt at present is absolutely dependent for fruitful existence, are interposed between it and the sea; while in lower latitudes still, where even the Sudan itself has scarcely been traversed, the arid country is in the hands of entirely savage people.

About 1,300 miles due south of the Egyptian boundary as the crow flies, Uganda and the Congo Free State form the southern frontier, the latter extending northwards to join the farthest and least-known confines of the French Sudan as the enclosing areas on the west, out of which appeared Marchand as "a bolt from the blue" on his way to Fashoda.

The whole importance of the country naturally depends on the river, which follows the great line of surface depression extending from Lake Nyassa to Syria and marked by the chain of Central African lakes, the Nile, and the Dead Sea. In the Sudan the retaining boundaries consist of the mountains of Abyssinia and of the Atbai district on the east, and the ridge on the west which separates Congo and Nile.

The drainage area of the Nile is divided into three great sections; the greatest extends far beyond the limits of the Sudan into the Uganda Protectorate, where the long-sought source was located as the Victoria Nyanza, the second into the Highlands of Abyssinia. The third, which is at present of least utilitarian importance, consists of the territory drained by the Bahr-el-Ghazal and its tributaries to the east of the Great Divide, from the western side of which many rivers flow into the Congo, and eventually into the Atlantic Ocean.

The general trend of the Nile to the northward is broken in one important and one minor instance.

Entering the Sudan at a point 4 degrees above the Equator it follows a rapid but tortuous course into the regions of swamp which characterize its most southerly section above the junction with the Bahr-el-Ghazal (this river being its first and only tributary on the west bank); it then takes a severe turn to the east, until once more deflected to its original direction by the flood with which the Sobat opposes it. North of Khartoum, in the Dongola province, it presents a remarkable divergence from its general course, assuming the form of the figure S on its side, the middle stretch actually flowing south-west for nearly 200 miles. During the whole of its course, the Nile only receives four tributaries of any importance—those on the east bank three in number, being the Atbara, north of Khartoum; the Blue Nile, on which Khartoum is situated; and the Sobat, far south, all taking their rise in Abyssinia.

Broadly speaking, the country might be divided into four sections: the desert of the north, the dry but inhabitable country of the west, the cultivatable areas of the centre and east, and the marshy, tropical regions of the south. But this classification, on more detailed examination, is subject to considerable modification.

In the north-west, away from the life-giving river which enriches the Dongola province, the country, almost entirely desert, is relieved by oases and peopled by nomad Arabs; while the district called the Atbai, in the extreme north-west bordering the Red Sea, while more or less desert in character, becomes mountainous, healthy, and has a rainfall during two months of the year which enables vegetation to exist in favoured spots. Through this district the Berber-Port Sudan railway runs to the Red Sea.

Kordofan in the west of the Sudan, on the left bank of the river, in common with Darfur on its remote side, has a considerable rainfall at one season, but the land soaks it up like a sponge. The country is characterized by groups of considerable hills, which in Darfur rise to a height of about 6,000 feet. Facing Kordofan, on the east of the river south of Khartoum, is the rich-soiled Ghezireh, flat, with occasional hills, backed by the district of the Blue Nile and tributaries, and with the Kassala province still farther behind, bordering Abyssinia, in all of which there is land of great fertility adapted to the cultivation of cotton or grain, and only waiting for water.

South of Kordofan and the Sobat, 500 miles upstream from Khartoum, is the land of superfluity, where water constitutes an *embarras de richesse*, and the country suffers in consequence. Here are thousands of square miles of swamps, the highest land in amongst them rising only a few feet above water-level, intersected by the Rivers Zeraf, Mountain Nile, and the system of the Bahr-el-Ghazal.

When, in the course of a journey up some branch of the latter river, whose ramifications extend over the whole province, the lowest-lying area is passed, a tropical country is entered which is favourable to the growth of fine timber, and, still more important, is situated within the zone suitable for the planting of rubber, in the cultivation of which important experiments are being made.

The Blue Nile and the Atbara both rise in the neighbourhood of Lake Tsana, far up in Abyssinia, and at the point of its entrance the former, with some hundreds of miles of its course still before it, is only 150 miles distant from the main stream of the White Nile.

For administrative purposes the country is divided into thirteen provinces, of which the most important are those of Dongola, Berber, and Khartoum, in the north; Sennaar and Kassala in the east; Kordofan in the west; and the Upper Nile and Bahr-el-Ghazal in the south. The chief towns of these are, respectively, Merowe, El Damer, Khartoum, Singa, Kassala, El Obeid, Kodok, and Wau. Dueim, the gate of Kordofan, is a flourishing port; but Omdurman, originally containing a vast population, decreases in numbers, while Khartoum North expands daily with the increase of commerce and occupation.

The tide of population and trade during ages gone by has come in from the east, as in Europe, and Asia overflowed into Africa by at least two well-defined routes, an important one being through Axum in Abyssinia, the other following the line of least resistance by the course of the river from Egypt.

From time immemorial the vast areas south of Upper Egypt have been known as the "Country of the Blacks," and from time immemorial they have been invaded by the peoples from the north, and have paid heavy toll in human flesh and gold. We find the first direct mention of them in a record of the Egyptian King Seneferu, probably 3766 B.C., first of the rulers of the Fourth Dynasty, whose militant spirit caused him to send a conquering army into the arid lands of the Ta-Nehesu nearly 4,000 years before Christ.

Yet in the time of the First Dynasty these areas must have been traversed to remote limits, as mention is made of the bringing of a pigmy captive to Memphis; and in these days it would appear that the pigmies extended into the country north of the Bahr-el-Ghazal, now held by Shilluks.

The thin line of the river and a chain of oases indissolubly connected the barbarism of the South with the civilization of the opulent North, yet in its history there are a few huge gaps which are only explainable by inferences from the local conditions of Egypt during these times. Monuments of stone tell stories of the victories of Egyptian

BUZ NYAL LEADS A FEMALE CHOIR.

arms, and the destruction and captivity of thousands of these negroes. Negroes, many of them, there undoubtedly were, their representations in the picture stories of Egypt faithfully demonstrating it.

Just as the Sudanese battalions of to-day fight for the cause of Egypt in the Sudan, so under the Sixth Dynasty, say 3230 B.C., did the aboriginals aid Pepi I., whose pyramid may be seen at Sakkara, to raid and harry the dwellers in the desert; and his general in later years may be judged, by his building of boats, to have penetrated far into the upper reaches of the White or Blue Niles, where suitable timber was, and still is, plentiful.

Ivory, ebony, gold, precious stones, frankincense, hides, and slaves, were brought by traders or victorious generals to add to the riches of Egypt, and during the decline of the Kings of Memphis, from the Sixth to the Twelfth Dynasties, until the ultimate rise of those of Thebes several hundred years later, while traders no doubt pursued their calling, the internal troubles of Egypt caused the Sudan to be left to itself. The history of these days being usually chronicles of exploits and victories, the silence of this great hiatus points naturally to the absence of military effort or of exploration.

Under the Theban Kings Egypt renewed her strength, and Menthuhetep III., taking his cue from the first of his name (Eleventh Dynasty), is depicted as the victor over the southern hordes, and the Kings of the Twelfth Dynasty (2466 B.C.

onwards) pursued with vigour their work of conquering and raiding the country, exacting tribute, and paying particular attention to the gold-mines.

Usertsen III. (2333 B.C.), the fifth King of the Twelfth Dynasty, established his authority as far south as Semneh, south of Wady Halfa, which he strongly fortified, as may be seen to this day, guarding the north from any incursion of the swarthy southern race. Indeed, it is probable that his influence extended farther south than this, and even to the Red Sea, so that the occupation, though of a continuously hostile country, was very complete.

The establishment of chains of forts, with the provision of temples, irresistibly reminds one of the stone ruins of Mashonaland, where the conditions appear to have been very similar. There, too, were alien invaders seeking gold in a hostile country, constructing chains of forts along their route, and with the great temple of Zimbabwe in their principal trade centre. But the opinion of some learned Egyptologists, though disputed by others, nevertheless condemns the Rhodesian ruins to an almost modern epoch, and Monomotapa is made infantile to Napata, in spite of the features they possess in common.

After a further blank in its history during the domination of Egypt by the Shepherd Kings, from the Fifteenth to the Seventeenth Dynasties, further expeditions took place from 1700 B.C. onwards, under the Eighteenth Dynasty, of which the records are more detailed, and speak of the native tribes, the Anti (hill-men) and Kensetin (cattle-men), who were encountered.

Remembering the recent history of Egypt and the Sudan, it appears but a repetition of its experiences in those far-away days, for when Amasis I. had conquered the cattle-rearing countries of the south, and had returned to Egypt, a prototype of the Mahdi arose, who, preaching a primitive *jehad*, victoriously attacked the strong forts at Semneh and elsewhere, and carried destruction to temples and their contents; but, in common with a successor, the Khalifa of his day, he eventually yielded to the superior power from the north.

Of the Kings of this dynasty, Thotmes III. appears to have most vigorously asserted the domination of Egypt, and the divisions of the Sudan are now first named.

His aunt, Queen Hatshepset, whose temple is to this day the most lovely sight at Deir-el-Bahari, Thebes, had sent an expedition by ship down the Red Sea, and inland into Punt, a name given to the territory stretching, probably, from the south of Khartoum to the Red Sea, and prolific in all the products of the Sudan, there found in abundance, such as gum, ebony, ivory, antimony, and wild animals.

Under Thotmes III. one might well speak of the "Egyptian Empire," extending its limits as it did, by virtue of his conquests, from the Euphrates to regions beyond Uauat (Northern Nubia), Kush (the country north of Khartoum), and yet again

Punt; for Punt was brought into such submission by him that she sent her tribute into Egypt by her own messengers, just as the Shilluks now bring their corn as tax to Fashoda.

The reign of his successor was remarkable for the first mention of the city of Napata (1500 B.C.), near Merawi, in what is now the province of Dongola, and for an activity in building, which was continued by later Kings of the dynasty.

The colony of Napata seems to have been located in fruitful soil, for it flourished exceedingly, and in the course of 500 years, reinforced by the priests dislodged from Thebes (966 B.C.), and identifying itself more or less with the races it was planted amongst, it waxed strong and healthy, aided by the natural resources and riches of its land. So strong, indeed, did it become that it succeeded in wresting the country as far as Assuan from the hands of the Egyptians, and about 734 B.C. Piankhi, King of Napata, in the weak period of the Twenty-third and Twenty-fourth Dynasties, actually forced his way to Memphis and annexed the whole land of Egypt.

Thus for a short period of ninety years Egypt existed under Ethiopian Kings, four in number, who were then brought into contact with Assyria and Judah, and gained the distinction of appearing in Old Testament history. Hezekiah, King of Judah, had had the misfortune to be defeated at Jerusalem by Sennacherib, and lost all his wives and concubines, with much treasure into the bargain. There appears to be a little confusion as to whether it were Shabataka, the second of the dynasty, or Taharq, the third, who came to the rescue by creating a diversion which led to Sennacherib's withdrawal. The Old Testament (Kings ii. 19) has it that it was Tirhakah, but it is possible that he was merely acting as general at a period prior to his accession.

The acquaintance of Hezekiah with the Ethiopians was apparently continued by his people, for the prophet Zephaniah, 621 B.C., who was son of *Cushi* and a great-great-grandson of a Hezekiah who was probably not the King, speaks with knowledge of the characteristics of Ethiopia: "From beyond the rivers of Ethiopia my suppliants, even the daughters of my dispersed, shall bring me offering" (Zeph. iii. 10). Can the word "dispersed" refer to the various armies which had suffered defeat by Assyrians?

The name *Cushi*, too, is interesting in this conjunction, through its contemporariness in regard to connection with these ancient inhabitants of Cush or Ethiopia, though indeed the Canaanites, being also descendants of Ham, have an ancestral connection with the eldest son, Cush, of the latter.

To return to the direct historical line, apart from Napata, we come about 1400 B.C. to days coincident with those of the history of the Israelites in Egypt, the days of the Rameses.

Nothing memorable took place until that great warrior and boaster Rameses II. came to the throne, and commemorated his victories by building or excavating temples, notable amongst which is that marvellous work, the temple of Abu Simbel, north of Wady Halfa, where, it is worthy of notice, may be seen representations of the swarthy inhabitants of the south.

Josephus, it is interesting to note (" Ant.," ii. 10), states that Moses, before initiating the enterprise so familiarly associated with his name, while a youthful and handsome man, headed an expedition against the kingdom of Meroe, and was received with open arms by the Sudanese Princess or Queen, Tharbis, who, falling a victim to beauty rather than to prowess, opened the gates of her capital to the brilliant young man, and won a moral victory by marrying him.

The expedition is confirmed by tradition quoted by the Arab historians Abu Salih and Selim-el-Aswam, who speak of his success against Tafa, forty miles above Assuan, and his marriage inferentially is testified to by Miriam and Aaron (Num. xi. 1), who were apparently jealous of him and objected to his influence, for had he not stooped to marry an *Ethiopian* woman ?

The only argument approaching solidity against the story of Josephus is that his wife, Zipporah, married when he fled from Egypt, and a Midianite of the Sinaitic peninsula, descendant of Shem, might generically on a basis improbably correct, and sarcastically as a term of reproach, have been styled " Ethiopian," even as Lord Salisbury is said to have called the white-skinned Mr. Dadabhai

Naoroji a "black man"; moreover, the name Tharbis does not appear on any monumental records, but this is not necessarily important. Later on in the Christian era the stretch north of Tafa is said to have been peopled by a Himyaritic race originating in Yemen, Southern Arabia, with which country and with Egypt the Midianites had intimate trade connections.

Once again the wave of Egyptian influence abated, and gradually weakened until the advent of Piankhi, when Egypt fell to Ethiopia.

After the eventual defeat and flight of Taharka, the third of the dynasty, by the Assyrians, when he lost Memphis and Thebes in the seventh century B.C., his stepson Tanuath-Amen, on his death, proclaimed himself King and re-occupied Thebes and Memphis, ejecting the Assyrians.

This proved unpopular with these enterprising aliens, who returned in numbers 660 B.C., and the subsequent history of Tanuath-Amen and the Ethiopian dynasty is indicated by the latter half of his name, so far as Egypt is concerned.

Relations with Egypt appear to have been slight for 200 years, and the exertions of the rulers were absorbed in extending and securing their dominions. But this period was remarkable for the accession of Egyptian blood in the reign of Psammeticus I., the following King (Twenty-sixth Dynasty), through the revolt of Egyptian troops stationed at Assuan, who were recompensed with the country of a disaffected tribe, twelve days south of Meroe—which is chronicled by Herodotus, who lived about 430 B.C.; also for the despatch of ambassadors to the Ethiopians by Cambyses, of the Twenty-seventh Dynasty (527 B.C.), followed by an abortive expedition against them. By this time Meroe, the site of which has been located near Shendi, had become the capital of the southern half of the kingdom, and the gold which is found in modern days in the higher portion of the Blue Nile indicates the locality where much of the loot of their expeditions came from.

The mantle of Piankhi descended by many Nubian Kings, of whom little is known, to a long line of Queens who were remarkable, as is shown by their representations at the temple of Nagaa, north of Khartoum, and elsewhere, for an amplitude of build often seen amongst the Bantu tribes of South Africa, but very seldom in the Sudan.

A representation in Dr. Wallis Budge's handbook on the Nile illustrates a female figure with characteristics particularly resembling those of a Pondo girl (South Africa), whose proportions commended themselves extravagantly to her swarthy admirers.

This series of Queens, who evidently ruled for some hundred years, appear invariably to have taken the name of Candace, for one hears of a Queen contemporary to Alexander the Great, who seems to have held her in a wholesome awe; and of others through the Ptolemaic period to the Roman and the Christian era, there being mention of them in Acts viii. 27. This speaks of the journey of a eunuch of authority under Candace, Queen of Ethiopia, who had charge of her treasure, who came to Jerusalem to worship, and was baptized at his own suggestion by Philip. If he safely returned, this is noteworthy as constituting the first entry of Christianity into the Sudan, a movement which afterwards attained great proportions.

The rule of these Queens and the preceding Kings was remarkable for considerable activity in building — many temples, monuments, and pyramids, existing at Meroe, Nagaa, Amara, and Soba, near Khartoum, which, while not exhibiting the degree of Egyptian excellence, are of great merit. The representations of Kings and Queens demonstrate in many cases distinctly negro characteristics, and one of the most interesting is the sculptured portrait of Candace, Queen Amen-Tarit, in her temple at Nagaa, found by Lepsius.

The days of the Ptolemies were mainly peaceful in the Sudan, and apart from the hunting of elephants, and insignificant building and additions to temples, they appear to have been confined to trade.

The Romans, having conquered Egypt, quickly came into collision with the dark races of the south. Candace—perhaps Queen Amen-Tarit—about 24 B.C. seized a psychological moment to attack Syene, the present Assuan. Success was not for long; her army was dispersed and taken, and Augustus Cæsar's victorious general, Petronius, forced his way actually to Napata, which he razed before retiring.

Nero despatched two centurions and soldiers to report on the Sudan, and they even appear to have reached the districts of the "sudd," which they faithfully describe; indeed, it is not by any means certain that they did not approach within measurable distance of the Great Lakes, for they describe fierce rapids which only exist near the exit of the Nile, and mention to Seneca the location of the "Nili Paludes" as under the "Mountains of the Moon."

The Alexandrian geographer Ptolemy, 150 A.D., correctly divined the sources of the Nile.

The Romans, however, never made any serious occupation of the Sudan. They added some temples, and, generally content with safeguarding Upper Egypt, merely put a heavy hand down on their turbulent neighbours when necessity arose.

The bugbears of the ancient Egyptians, the Anti, became known as the Blemmyes, and spread into Upper Egypt. Diocletian (284 A.D.) brought diplomacy into play, and secured the assistance of the Blemmyes by a payment similar to the British subsidy to the Ameer of Afghanistan, and cemented the arrangement by an agreement with another warlike tribe, the Nubæ, or Nobatæ, who were enlisted to watch the Blemmyes, and were probably blacks from the west bank. By the year 580 A.D., in the reign of Tiberius II., the Roman rule had practically come to an end.

Considering the fanatical character of the religion

PHILÆ: AN IMMEMORIAL FRONTIER POST.

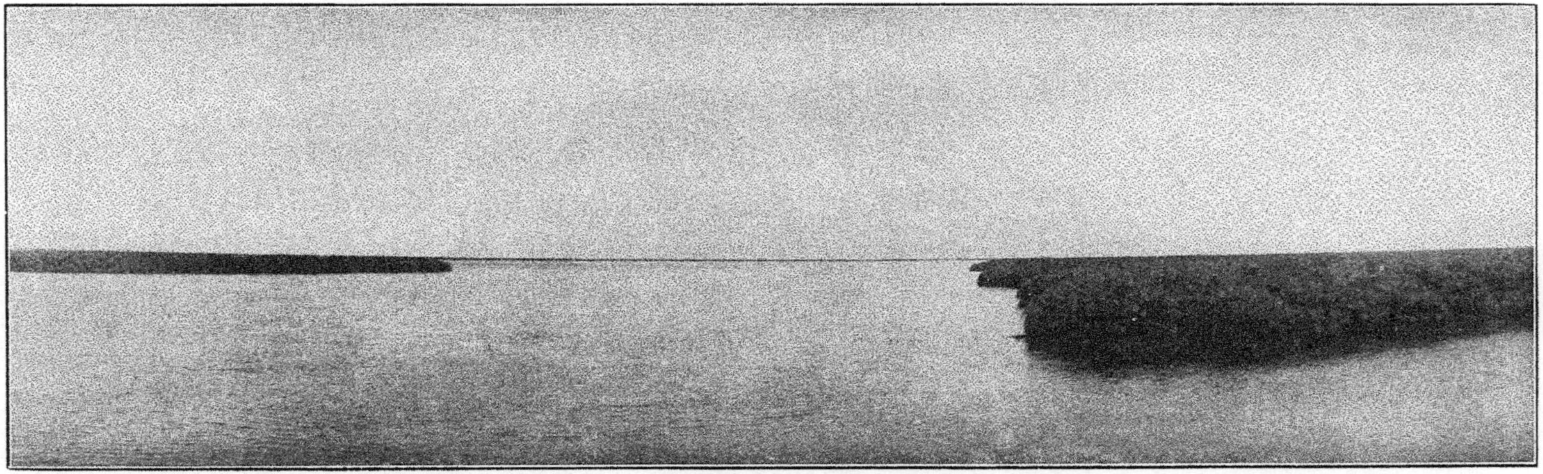

LAGOON IN THE "SUDD."

To face page 26.

of the Sudan at the present day, the fact that the country became a Christian one in the latter half of the sixth century, during the decadence of Roman influence, is remarkable. And that Christianity should have spread with such rapidity, through savage hordes, into regions so far removed from the then modern civilization, is yet more extraordinary.

But it must not be forgotten that there was already a basis on which to work. The heathen and savage were not unleavened. The colonies of ancient Egyptians, however completely they may seem to have vanished, had their influence; the exiled Theban priests of Amen-Ra transplanted a religious atmosphere, and though their line terminated about 200 A.D., there are evidences that a century later their religion still existed.

For over 200 years before this, Christianity had taken root in Egypt, and St. Mark is supposed to have led the movement for many years there, if, indeed, not farther south also. The news of salvation forced its way past Roman persecution and Egyptian superstition, over hungry deserts, mid heathen tribes, with the resistless penetration by which the tender seedling pushes its head through the hardest of surfaces.

Persecution drove the converts south along the line of least resistance, and the Blemmyes who were defying Diocletian may have harboured, or at least have tolerated, them.

By 330 A.D. Christianity had begun its invasion

of Ethiopia via Abyssinia as well, taking the old trade route, followed by Queen Hatshepset of the Eighteenth Dynasty, which had from the earliest days been the alternative to that of the Nile. Frumentius, later Bishop of Axum, having with a fellow-student been wrecked in the Red Sea, became tutor to the Queen's son, and founded a mission in Abyssinia, whose work, albeit corrupted, exists in full force to this day.

Exhibiting the vehemence with which religion appeals to the inhabitants of the Sudan, the wave swept over the country, and in the sixth century a Christian King, Silko (550 A.D.), converted by a missionary of the Empress Theodora, ruled from his headquarters at the historical seat of the Kings of old Dongola. As chief of the Nubæ, or Nobatæ, he was the hereditary enemy of the Blemmyes, and religious differences formed useful occasion for a warfare which ended in the delivering of the country between Assuan and Halfa from their control. Many Christian churches were built, the remains of a large number existing to this day, notably at Nagaa and Soba. Even Abu Simbel came into employment.

The connection between Silko and the north at this time receives interesting confirmation by the recent discovery at the old Coptic seat of Christianity, Edfu, in Upper Egypt, of an ancient book, believed to be in the Nubæ language, which is evidently a history of St. Mena, who, in his youth a Roman soldier, became a convert, and was martyred 307 A.D. at Almuna. The book, of eighteen pages, in vellum, $6\frac{1}{4}$ inches by 4 inches wide, was found in a cave in the desert near Edfu by a shepherd, and came into the possession of the British Museum. The language is unknown, though the characters are Greek, and thus resemble the inscriptions found at Soba, and perhaps at Geteina, according to Gleichen.

But only for a century did Christianity enjoy full sway, for the overwhelming advance of the Arab invasion placed its King under Mohammedan power.

The Mohammedan general Abdallah Bin Said, operating from Assuan after the conquest of Egypt, laid siege to Napata and defeated its King, Koleydozo, 651 A.D.

But absolute Arab dominion was not immediate: the victor contented himself with making a treaty ensuring the benevolent treatment of the Mohammedans, and regulating the conditions of entry by Nubæ into Egypt and by Mohammedans into Nubia; and for 600 years an annual tribute was paid.

During this period incursions were made into Egypt by the Nubians, with varying success, but in a manner which demonstrated their power even to the redoubtable Saladin.

The wars of the Crusades abating, Muslim energy was free to turn its attention to other quarters, and neglect to pay tribute formed sufficient excuse in 1275 A.D. for a successful expedition into Nubia, which resulted in much destruction of Coptic churches and in definite annexation, but for some hundred years more no backbone was put into its conquest.

The most serious shock came from within. A race came to the fore whose origin is hidden in doubt, a fact which tends in favour of its coming from other than Arab stock, and probably from the south or west. Certainly the Fung nation possesses characteristics which are not those of the Arab, and retains traces of customs, such as the use of the boomerang, which one is accustomed to associate with quite primitive peoples, and is depicted as in use by the ancient Anti against the early Egyptians. They are also addicted—as are the Azande of the south—to eating dog and pig flesh, abhorred of the faithful. Much of the journey described in the following pages passed through their country.

The Fungs began to crowd the Christian blacks of Meroe, coming from the eastward, and, operating from their capital Sennaar on the Blue Nile, expelled them from the large town Soba, near Khartoum. From the fourteenth to the eighteenth century the Fung dynasty was a paramount power, their territory extending from Abyssinia at one time to the frontier of Darfur, as for five years they held Kordofan. They dispossessed the Nubæ inhabitants of the Ghezireh who may have been added to those in the mountains of Kordofan, where the Nuba tribe, very black in skin, still exists in numbers.

Threatened about 1517 A.D. by an invasion through Abyssinia by Selim, the first Turkish Sultan to own Egypt, the wily Fung King, Amara Dunkas, had resource to artifice to preserve his nation, at the cost of any conscience he may have possessed. He succeeded in convincing Selim that he was a good Muslim, and his genealogical tree as an Arab filled Selim with amazement, and stupefies present-day genealogists. All of which goes to show Dunkas as a plausible diplomatist.

But this rang the knell of the Christian kingdom of Napata. Meroe was evacuated after hundreds of years of dignity, leaving only its monuments; Napata sank into obscurity, and the bulwark which for so long had delayed the spread of Mohammedanism over Africa succumbed to a flank attack.

Poncet, the first European of more modern days to visit the Sudan, gives evidence of the moral anarchy which ensued after the disruption of the Christian Church and the superficial absorption of Mohammedan tenets. He proceeded from Dongola in 1699, and on to Sennaar, in company with Father de Brevedent, one of that marvellous body which, 150 years before, had founded a Jesuit mission even at Zimbabwe in Mashonaland.

Under a series of competent rulers the Fung kingdom had progressed. Many missionaries, mainly Franciscan friars, who became responsible for the murder of M. le Noir du Roule by Badi-el-Ahmar in 1704, were in the country, and it is not surprising to learn that in the reign of Badi-el-Shilluk, 1724, after nearly 100 years of cultivated education, it was recognized, even in Constantinople, as a seat of learning, and Sennaar was visited by Oriental philosophers from many lands.

The Hamegs, whose descendants live side by side with those of the Fungs at the present day, eventually gained power, retaining it well on into the nineteenth century, when Ismail Pasha, accompanied by an American, extended Egyptian rule to the limits of Abyssinian territory at the bidding of his father, Mehemet Ali; Ibrahim, his brother, ascended the White Nile, and his brother-in-law, Mohammed, took Kordofan and Darfur, committing outrages out of the common even in the Sudan. It is interesting to read that, according to Sir H. H. Johnston, officers of the American army were employed also in later years by Gordon, the Khedive desiring the advantage of British characteristics in his officials, with the detachment of transoceanic nationality.

The modern history of the country is so well known through the writings of Bruce, Cailliaud, Baker, and others, including those of the period of the Mahdi rebellion, that it is unnecessary to refer to it in detail. Suffice it to add that during the next sixty years Egyptian rule was consolidated, after a successful fight with Abyssinia at Sennaar and fruitless rebellions at Kassala. Baker in 1870 extended it far to the south into Equatorial Africa, of which territory Gordon became Governor, the latter being appointed Governor-General of the entire Sudan in 1877.

The Mahdi arose in 1881, and Gordon, brought out of retirement to evacuate the Sudan in 1884, was murdered on the fall of Khartoum on January 26, 1885. In September, 1898, at the Battle of Omdurman, Kitchener opened the way to Khartoum, the last blow to Mahdism being given by the death of the Khalifa at Um Debreikat, inland, opposite Goz Abu Guma and the birthplace of Mahdism, on November 24, 1899.

It is patent that, however much light has been thrown on the history of the Sudan during recent years, incomplete as our knowledge is now, there is yet ample opportunity for further discovery of its more ancient history in the investigation of the monuments and in the study of the ethnological problems which abound.

CHAPTER III

IN A LAND DESERTED

THOSE who take pleasure in sport, natural history, the freedom of an unrestrained life out of doors, the study of unsophisticated man, or the development of a new country, cannot find a more favourable land for the indulgence of their fancy than the Sudan.

It was the combination of all these interests which had more than once drawn me thither, rather than any one in particular; and while sport claims the greatest attention on a journey up the Blue Nile and its affluents, man irresistibly obtrudes himself in less-known regions far south.

Khartoum, the base of all expeditions, is now under ten days' journey from London, and most sportsmen will find it convenient to be there before the end of the year, to allow for the making of preparations, and to obtain a start by the time the long grass has been at least partly burnt off. It is essential to arrange long beforehand for supplies of ammunition to be forwarded in advance, though some, of uncertain supply, can be obtained on the spot. Tents are unnecessary at this time of the year; an X bed is best, with valise for bedding and mosquito-curtains; and if much camel-riding be undertaken, it is well to be provided with a *maklufa*, or saddle, and with the large grass matting of the country, which best protects baggage from being frayed by the camel-hair ropes, and is also a means of obtaining shade by day, and of carpeting the rough ground by the bedside at night.

A donkey or mule, the latter in preference, is most useful when approaching spots favoured by game, and much tedious walking may thus be avoided.

Air-tight tin uniform cases are handy, and are well adapted for loading on the camel; while the wooden boxes specially made for the same purpose most efficiently carry food and kitchen utensils. Some use them for clothing as well.

Practically everything required can be obtained in Khartoum, and the sending of goods from England is costly or tedious, very probably both. Long mosquito-boots of soft leather are essential in the more southerly districts, and for the same reason I found loose leather gloves, covering the elbows, a useful protection; for the hands and elbows are liable to come into contact with the mosquito-nets, and it is wonderful to see with what celerity the insects instantly repair to the point where these touch.

The ·303 rifle is forbidden, for military reasons.

Servants are best engaged in Khartoum, and expect to be brought back there; a cook and *suffragi*, or personal attendant, should be sufficient.

Shikaris and guides are naturally engaged in the country visited.

The methods of travelling to Singa, the point of departure from the Blue Nile when following the Dinder upstream, are three in number. Up to December, or perhaps a little later, it can be reached by steamer; but this being earlier than most people would care to arrive, the alternative routes are by camel along the Blue Nile, the whole distance of 270 miles, or by steamer to Hillet Abbas (in the near future by rail on part of each route), thence on the camels, already ordered to be in attendance there, across the Ghezireh to Singa, only ninety-five miles away.

It was this route which I followed, and which proved a useful preparation for the subsequent journey, after good friends in the country, whose assistance was invaluable, and to whom many thanks are due, had been left far behind.

How many African travellers, when seated carelessly by the home fireside, allow their thoughts to wander back to the red embers of the camp-fire, the grey, ghostly forms of skeleton trees, the white cone of mosquito-curtained bed, and the motionless excrescences of shadow, denoting the resting camels or their dusky drivers? How inconsequentially, at odd moments during the night, occurs the sleepy-toned chatter of one camp-follower to another, a camel's grumble, or the far weird sounds of wild nature. The breeze fans the cheek, the stars are brilliant; above and around is darkness, the abode

GEBEL KORDI: A TYPICAL HILL 350 FEET HIGH.

THE BLUE NILE AT SINGA.

To face page 36.

of mystery, holding at close quarters one knows not what, and ready to close in and enfold the resting cosmos of humanity should the logs burn down and the firelight fail.

The hour is favourable to fancy, the imaginary assumes the cloak of reality, while reality becomes exaggeration. Even the dead silence enveloping the casual noises of camp and forest is invested with significance and causes awe. The immensity of the heavenly vault, the thick gloom of illimitable space surrounding, the freedom of the earth to everything nocturnal, encourage the reception of impressions which always remain fresh and enduring.

Seen 70 feet above from its precipitous bank, even in this dry season, the swift Blue Nile was great at Singa, following its own chosen path in the broad, yellow expanse of sand 270 miles above Khartoum. Ripples on its surface here and there denoted the presence of great fish. A narrow black head would show up for a moment, or a long, loathly body crawl out on the far side of the river, for the crocodile is not yet driven away. Strange and incongruous it seemed to see a steel boat push out to these same sand-banks, and the crocodiles give way to the children of the Egyptian Mamur for their afternoon's play.

In the evening the air became clamorous with the shouts of Arabs urging their camels into the craft by which they crossed the broad stream; the mule had gaily hopped into it and out again with little ado, and for a quarter of a mile all plodded the sandy width to the sudden, steep rise on the eastern side, which holds in check the turbulent torrent of the rainy season.

A momentary stop before plunging into the gloom of the bush topping the bank showed one the lights of the Sudanese township, representing the last touch of civilization before entering the confines of a depopulated country returned to the domination of the wild beast. The candle-light uncertainly showed the foot-tracks of the camels winding for a mile toward the great baobab or tebeldi tree (*Adansonia digitata*) which marked the first camping-ground.

Good-byes had been said, the drunken cook lectured, and only the few short hours of the night preluded the departure *on safaria*.

Regeneration is the watchword of this province of Sennaar. In early days the seat of a barbarian civilization and a learning which even called votaries from far India, it fell upon evil times. The capital of the Fung kingdom of Sennaar, founded in the sixteenth century, it successfully resisted the Abyssinian forces in 1719, but later Mehemet Ali reached out his conquering hand from Cairo, though suffering the loss of his son Ismail by treachery at Shendi in 1822. Egyptian forces held posts at Sennaar and Roseires, at which latter place may still be seen a battered band instrument of ante-Mahdi date.

Even in 1883 the Mahdists, under Ahmed Wad el Makashef, had besieged Sennaar town unsuccessfully, the siege being raised by that capable soldier, Abdel Kader Pasha.

Subsequently the Egyptians under Nur Bey were defeated and Sennaar burnt by El Mehrdi Abu Rof, who—says Ohrwalder—was actually a descendant of the ancient Kings of Sennaar, and chief of the powerful Gehena tribe, which for long defied the Mahdi's power.

Possession was regained by the Egyptians, and, on the rise of the Mahdi, Nur Bey conducted the famous defence of the town with 3,000 soldiers, undergoing a siege which terminated in August, 1885, seven months after the fall of Khartoum, 700 men alone remaining. Nur Bey, still living in Omdurman in 1892, escaped the fate of the defenders of Kassala, who were murdered a month later by Osman Digna (still irreconcilable and in captivity at Wady Halfa in 1909), on the fall of that last remaining post.

And what of the remains of the ancient kingdom of Sennaar after a few years of Dervish rule? The independence inherited of a line of rulers by El Mehrdi Abu Rof stirred him to resist the Mahdi, and his head soon rotted on Omdurman walls. His people were slaughtered in thousands, famine silenced the land, village upon village disappeared for ever, leaving merely a name to be heard by the white traveller of to-day. The granary of the Sudan was reduced to a howling wilderness, and its enfeebled remnants of population shrank to the narrowest limits.

So now the thousands of square miles ahead are but sparsely populated for the first few miles, and thereafter are merely names of habitations long disappeared, and subsisting only in memory or tradition.

Architectural landmarks in African history, apart from those under Egyptian influence, the foreign buildings of Zimbabwe in Mashonaland, and the more substantial Arab structures in the Western Sudan and Nigeria, are practically non-existent. Mud walls, if not continually repaired, are washed away by tropical rains, and honey-combed by bees or the busy mason-wasp. Wood falls a prey to termites and to rot, and the disappearance of mankind is followed with startling speed by the obliteration of all trace of his dwelling. Thus we are debarred from a great aid in the tracing of racial movements and origin.

It is unnatural and distasteful to rise before dawn, and the stifled yawns of the awakening Arabs annoy one. But the grumbling of camels and restlessness of a stirring camp rouse one effectually, and toilet is completed *en plein air*. Oh, the freshness of it! No confinement between four walls, no restricted atmosphere, the birds beginning to call around one, life awakening everywhere, one feels thus part and parcel of the world of living creatures, not a detached, imprisoned being, half bereft of the senses we were originally provided with, through sheer lack of opportunity to use.

The whole company is Arab, but Arab of various

SUDAN RESIDENCES: OLD AND NEW STYLE.

FIRST SIGHT OF THE DINDER: KHAMISA.

To face page 40.

sorts and colours; a shikari, Ibrahim, his relative Abdullah and two youths, Fadl el Mullah and Abdullah Bachit the younger, come as helpers; Abid the cook and Mustapha the valet see to personal effects, while various camel-drivers of skimpy attire quarrel over the loads, and manage their awkward charges with precision and dexterity.

The camel provides an object-lesson in specialization by nature, so curiously does he fulfil particular requirements of mankind in particular circumstances, and so excellently is he provided with mechanical and mental arrangements for fulfilling the same objects. The provision of extra stomachs for the purpose of carrying a water-supply is his most famous attribute, but there are many others which are only apparent when actual use is made of his services. Even his wife has the virtue of providing an excellent milk, highly appreciated by connoisseurs.

The peculiar jointing of his legs enables his body to be easily amenable to loading, his hump serves the double purpose of being a reservoir of nutritive fat in days of scarcity and a convenient projection for attachment of the saddle. As he squats on the ground with legs neatly folded, a useful hardened pad on the lower part of his chest takes the main portion of his weight, and his front leg and neck form convenient stepping-places for making an ascent to the saddle.

His feet are soft pads, and splay over the yielding sand as he gently places them; he keeps up his slow, steady pace hour after hour if a baggage camel, and trots his easy, sliding step if a riding one. His hair provides the material for the ropes which enthral him, and his dung, in default of wood, a useful fuel. He is guided by a pat on either side of the neck; a rope round his muzzle, with a thin string threaded through the skin of the nostril, gives some control. Hurry is foreign to the baggage camel's nature, deliberation of a supercilious kind the main point in his creed.

Yet this admirable animal has his drawbacks. He can take nothing cheerfully; he labours under a feeling of continual injustice; he growls when he is loaded; it is equally an imposition on his good-nature when he is relieved of his burden. He takes a delight in grabbing at his rider when mounting into the saddle, and rejoices in rising suddenly before it is safely entered. And the rising of a camel is (to the rider) a matter of moment: first, the sudden tilting back as he gets to his knees, next, an equally violent thrust forward as the hind-legs come into action, and then back once again.

On the march he loves to be the last of the file; he avails himself of every opportunity of unexpectedly swinging aside a couple of yards of neck to pluck a mouthful of desiccated thorns; he picks out the worst of the path so that he may have an excuse for stumbling (and a ten-foot stumble is no joke); he drops on every possible occasion into the walk which renders the deficiency of a waist joint obvious in the human frame; he is the prey of huge ticks; and lastly, and above all, he stinks. The sweat-gland at the back of his head would be well placed for him if he appreciated the odour as does the European, and no wonder that game fly at his approach within a mile or so.

The traveller is well advised each night to ascertain the direction of the wind, as otherwise he will find that his camel-drivers have thoughtfully placed their property in the most advantageous position for assuring him of its presence.

Equally strange are the owners. A class apart, half the year they are nomads, journeying hither and thither, onward or homeward as business leads them, they and their camels becoming almost part of each other. They sleep together; the man will share his dhurra with his *alter ego*, and will grumble and complain identically.

The camel-driver is a race to himself; ordinarily small and slight, often with pronounced Semitic features, he is of the lowest order of Arab intelligence, yet with the sharpened instincts and the endurance of primitive life. Fortified with one skin full of dhurra, and another of water, he will travel hundreds of miles, sometimes by day, at others by night, when he sings alternately with his companions along the straggling line to insure cohesion, and to scare wild beasts from the line of march.

An unaccustomed mule with an unfamiliar saddle proved to be inferior in comfort to the easy trotting camel, and twenty miles of riding over rough tracks with a saddle too much arched proved a trial even to one already well broken in to African journeying.

It is a good rule to see the baggage camels off early on their way to the midday halting-place, so that lunch may be awaiting one after a morning's stalk; and never is it so fully realized how long is a stern chase than when, hot and weary, the tracks of these "tortoises" are followed with the knowledge that refreshment and siesta ensue on their overhauling.

This twenty miles lay between the Blue Nile and its tributary, the River Dinder, much of the way being by a new track through thick bush, offering every variety of jolt through the virgin roughness of the ground. The native town of Khamisa gave the first sight of the Dinder through a break in the vegetation, now merely a stream of sand with large deep pools at intervals, sometimes under the precipitous bank on this side, or stretching across to overhanging jungle opposite. The Dinder joins the Blue Nile 180 miles south-east of Khartoum, and the more easterly Rahad comes in at Wad Medani, forty miles lower down. The general flow of all three rivers is north-west, and divergence in the direction of their sources is very gradual.

The African robin, black with scarlet breast, peeped at the white man resting in the shade; small monkeys carefully crawled down to the water's edge, scared quickly by the slightest movement; while elsewhere little children drove sheep and goats to water down the steep incline.

The journey onwards to Abu Hashim provided a lesson in the utility of a common language. Ibrahim had failed to learn Esperanto; my Arabic was yet of the most limited scope. All had heard at Singa of the number of elephants beyond Abu Hashim, that had been causing consternation to the villagers.

The path was suddenly broken by a deep gorge, with sides so crumbling and precipitous that the passage of camels seemed a sheer impossibility. The mule found little difficulty though dislodging much soil, and the first camel, relieved of its load, plunged, still disdainfully, into the abyss, clambering on its knees up the friable ledges, and gaining the top after much groaning and fuss. Under circumstances such as these one learns to appreciate the virtue of patience, for it was long before the passage of the Khor Agaliin was effected, and the camels once more loaded.

In the meantime my eye rested on a large, irregular oval impression on the dusty ground; the surface was smooth, yet traversed by veinlike markings. Other and yet other ovals surrounded it, and the memories of a chase in a distant country, far up on the Mountain Nile, came back to me. *Fil* (elephant), smiled Ibrahim, breaking in on my thoughts; and onward as we travelled more numerous and fresh became the great tracks, while broken branches and heaps of fresh dung showed how recent was the presence of the mighty herd.

Villagers passed, and conversation took place; they came with donkeys—as I thought, *en route* for their hut villages. "A plague on Babel!" thought I, as Ibrahim talked earnestly to me. We pressed forward, and only that night did I learn that the Inspector who had preceded me on a local visit that afternoon had met and killed his first elephant within a mile of the spot. Far away by this time was the herd, leaving one, fortunately, with the tiny ·303 bullet in his brain to provide food for scores of villagers, who flocked like vultures to the kill.

The dissection and division of the carcass is one of the revolting sights of Africa, for brute man swarms in and around it, recking nothing of the gore, and finding fruitful cause of quarrel.

The tusks, brought in to Abu Hashim at night, made their presence known by an elephantine odour, and presented the characteristics of those of the Blue Nile as contrasted with the giants of the White Nile, being of 30 and 34 pounds weight only. It is difficult to account for the difference in size existing within so comparatively small a distance, as distances in Africa go, but variations in other animals appear in much the same way. For example, the maneless lion is common in this district, whereas farther south the mane is almost invariable. Moreover, one gathers that the Somaliland lion is of a more enterprising character in regard to human meat than his brother of the Sudan, who, as a rule, will let mankind alone if

CROSSING THE KHOR AGALIIN.

A GIANT TEBELDI-TREE.

To face page 46.

let alone himself. In Southern Africa, also, the lion has to be taken more into consideration, though in my solitary experience there of meeting one, when armed with a twenty-bore shot gun, he fortunately rejected his opportunity.

The Blue Nile and Dinder are certainly remarkable for an occasional picturesqueness, for the most part absent on the White Nile, which, owing to its great width, dwarfs the height of banks and bush or forest that in a smaller river have more influence on the landscape. At the wide sweeping bends of the stream this was particularly the case, when the water was blue in the late afternoon, and the latent colours of the country were freed from the binding thraldom of the tyrannous sun.

Quite a typical scene of this description is supplied by the small village of Durraba, 70 feet above the bank, at a majestic curve, the last post of even Arab civilization in this deserted country, where a few families were making a hard fight against drought and famine.

During the previous day we had met many small parties on their way down-river, consisting of families travelling to other localities to obtain scanty supplies of dhurra (Indian millet, or sorghum, the staple food of the Sudan), the crop of which had failed in this district.

Yet Sir Samuel Baker, passing only fifty miles away in 1861, reported the neighbouring country of the Rahad to be full of Arabs, with abundant supplies of corn.

For 100 miles before us, in ante-Mahdi days, there had been village upon village, the more distant of them, it is true, being retired from on the approach of the wet season. Now all have disappeared, save a police post at Khor Galegu and a slavery post on the Abyssinian frontier.

The Sheikh of Durraba made the inevitable mistake of the African native, and called for my services as a doctor. On receiving sufficient medicine for five white men, impatient for a cure, he disregarded my instructions, and took it all at once, leaving me with an uneasy conscience for many days after.

Poor as they were—perhaps anticipatory of vast loads of dried meat to come to them as a result of my chase—they were painstaking for my comfort, and hospitable.

It had not been brewing-day, and so the usual offering of merissa or um-bil-bil was not forthcoming. Moreover, it was not a land of plenty, but I was provided with a cool, thirst-quenching decoction, consisting of flakes of treated dhurra flour steeped in a great preponderance of water.

At Abu Hashim, the handsome and intelligent Egyptian Mamur, Achmet Khalil, sighing in his loneliness for the fleshpots of Egypt, had laughingly caused one of his subordinates to bring me samples of the already familiar merissa, and of its refinement um-bil-bil, which is manifestly superior, in that it is less disagreeable.

In the weeks to come I was to be made aware

of the qualities of merissa in a still more pronounced way than had occurred at the start of my journey from Singa on the Blue Nile, where my otherwise more or less virtuous cook had become a chronic nuisance to the neighbourhood.

To the average Englishman who has not strayed from the hedge-confined country of his own land, it is a little difficult to form a mental picture of the unrestricted wildness of the African landscape. Yet I have seen spots in Scotland which might well have been in the Sudan, and stretches of park-like, finely-timbered land in Mid-Africa which might equally well have surrounded one of the stately homes of England.

In Rhodesia I have suddenly emerged from thick bush into such an expanse of country, the long, sun-dried, yellow grass evenly covering an undulating park, dotted, as if by an expert landscape gardener with clumps of trees or wide-spreading single ones in elegant positions.

But in the Sudan such spots are rare. The country, as a rule, is either too dry during a great portion of the year, or, farther south, in the great swampy regions, too wet. It is annually devastated by destructive grass fires, which scorch and stunt the trees, leaving the deep-seated grass roots unharmed, and manured by the salts of the burnt ash.

So the greater part of the bush consists of numberless small, straggly specimens of the various acacias, sunt, hashab, talh, and kuk, which produce gum arabic; and the fruit-trees (*sic*), heglig and nabbuk. In certain favoured spots one will find the sunt (*Acacia arabica*) particularly well grown, and the wood, though hard, is in demand as timber and firewood.

Here and there one will meet specimens, usually solitary or small in number, of the few trees which are stout enough to resist the mighty strength of the elephant: the baobab or tebeldi tree, often 30 or 40 feet round, useless as timber; the tall kuk-tree; and the tamarind, with its medicinal fruit and welcome shade.

The cheerful Fadl el Mullah betook himself to my instruction in the attributes of many objects, handing me an excess of the small round fruit of the nabbuk, whose stone is surrounded by a friable substance of neutral taste, which came in useful on at least one occasion, when a meal was in the far distance.

Many voided stones in the tracks of elephants showed the partiality of the great beast for the date-like fruit of the heglig, called *lalub* by my Arabs. The stone is large, and under a tough skin is covered with a bitter-sweet, astringent substance, which is also esteemed by the natives medicinally, while the kernel is productive in oil.

Parties passed *en route* had reported much game ahead, but such reports are highly unreliable as a rule, and made in order to please, for the moment, the unsophisticated among sportsmen.

The course of the Dinder here is erratic in the extreme, winding and bending round upon itself in the way which a river in the flat Sudan country so well knows how to exhibit. So a trek across country is made, and the difference in luxuriance of vegetation is instantly manifest. The bush becomes thinner, and the grass is long and overwhelms everything. Vast areas have already been burnt, and the ash partially hides the multitudinous cracks in the friable "cotton soil," rendering walking difficult and mule-riding a torture owing to continual stumbles.

This soil is one of the peculiarities of the district; scarcely a square foot of it is without a deep fissure interlacing itself with others, and the islets crumble away under one's weight. In the rainy season it must be almost impassable, and many a time and oft are to be seen the huge pits caused by elephants' feet sinking deep in the course of their meanderings.

Here we took our first long walk, the mule and donkey being led gently some distance behind, ready to stop at an instant's warning on game being sighted. It was early in the morning, and the forest resounded with the voices of birds, almost startling in their strangeness and variety. From one quarter came the shrill, commanding call of a policeman's whistle; everywhere sounded the word *catecherak* (Arabic equivalent for "thank you"), repeated with emphasis until the very idea of gratitude became nauseous; the crows uttered their strange conversation, varying from a bubbling noise to a squawk and a double note in minor thirds, while another whistle resembled an interrogative

"Who are you?" Oribi gazelle leapt, and, slim as greyhounds, darted among bushes and grass tufts—on one occasion failing to do so before a bullet had laid a pretty creature low.

As the sun crept higher in the heavens the bird-voices gradually ceased, walking became more onerous, and the canvas bag of cold tea carried by the mule was much sought after.

But heat, thirst, and fatigue, were on the instant forgotten when Ibrahim, peeping over the river-bank, was seen to crouch suddenly low, signalling wildly for my approach, then stealthily raising his head to keep his eye on a moving black line of animals some hundreds of yards up the river-bed. "Gamoos" (buffalo), whispered Ibrahim. As we looked they trotted slowly up a large *khor*, and we retreated hastily, to take a short cut to intercept them. Descending into the river-bed, where the heat radiated from the sand was terrific, we followed the tracks into a large extent of grass which towered above our heads. Here our passage was only made possible by the fact that our quarry had passed before, and we emerged, covered with crawling, black grass ticks, to find it had vanished beyond the bank into the recesses of the bush, where we failed to overtake it.

I lay exhausted under a tree while word was sent back to camp for lunch, regardless of the fact that the ground was soft with black ashes; little cared I for the colour of my clothes. Ibrahim, also half dead with thirst, still employed himself by seeking and returning with that mocker of a dried-up palate—wild honey, Just as we fail to locate a face in an unexpected spot, which would be immediately named in its own surroundings, so were the contents of a bottle brought by Abid a matter of speculation to me. Taking a long and thirsty draught, I was instantly aware that it was some strange and unaccustomed beverage. An inquiring look brought from Abid the remark, "Sherba," and I awoke to the fact that, taken in bulk, one discovers an entirely different—and unpleasing—impression of the desirability of *soup*.

A leopard made his presence known at night, and the fires were more carefully attended to, though it was noticeable that as the journey wore on, even though lion paid us attention, the men grew more and more careless in keeping the fires bright. Weird are the night noises of the bush, and one falls asleep trying to translate them.

Climatic conditions vary here as elsewhere: one day is sultry and oppressive in its shimmering, burning stillness; on another a cool breeze robs the sun-heat of its scorch and puts elasticity into one's limbs. Even the soft sand of the river-bed seems less impeding, and energy revives.

Near Kantarow we passed through *khors* where the forest was very thick, and old elephant spoor was visible everywhere. A reed-buck lost the protection of its colour by venturing on an area of black, burnt land, but retired into long elephant grass on observing me in a like predicament.

Time after time, travelling well back from the bank, a cautious peep was given over its brink, and at last a herd of ariel (Soemmering's gazelle) showed up unexpectedly on the other side of a long pool, but out of range. Large crocodiles slid into the water as they sighted us, but the lust of the chase rendered them unattractive.

Far across, in the midst of the river of sand—here perhaps half a mile wide—was a stranded tree, brought down by the summer floods and left at the edge of the water. I crossed laboriously to it, finding a snug retreat under its fallen trunk and branches which demonstrated a prior occupant. Much buck spoor was to be seen around it, but on the moister sand of the pool limit was the impression of the great pad of the King of Cats, fresh as if just made. I had inadvertently stumbled upon a lair where lion could lie at ease in wait for the antelope as they came for their daily drink.

The far side was densely wooded, and the guinea-fowl scuttled away in hundreds as passage was slowly made through it. For the time I was alone, and at length rested quietly for my men to arrive. It was well that this was so, for, becoming aware of movement in the bush, I glanced up to see, stringing slowly through the tangle of vegetation, a herd of the lovely ariel. So charming was the sight that I was reluctant to spoil it, and watched the first few pass before I awoke to a sense of my needs. Firing at one, which fell dead, I kept still while the herd first gazed astonished, searching for the enemy, and as I pressed the trigger a second time the bush became alive with the graceful forms, two remaining behind.

The Arabs hurried to the spot at the sound of the shots. Ibrahim, Fadl el Mullah, and Abdullah exploded with hysterics of delight, giving vent to howls and yells which conveyed the tidings of this very unextraordinary success to the camel-drivers a mile away. The throats of the animals were cut before I could get up to them. No matter how often one may tell one's shikaris, they will inevitably cut them close to the jaw if one be not present in time, and such was the case in this instance.

Fat as butter and as heavy as a man, they were soon skinned and dressed and *en route* for camp on a camel's back ; but the fat from the back above the tail was taken out and roasted instantly, proving not altogether untasty in this land of lean food.

CHAPTER IV

SPORT BY THE RIVER

FADL EL MULLAH, the cheerful fool, was full of good intentions as a result of the prospect of a meat dinner. He filled my pockets with nabbuk fruit, and picked the grass ticks off my clothes before they had time to burrow their heads into my skin. It is somewhat of a puzzle to account for the existence of so many myriads when one estimates the chance of an individual tick finding a suitable lodging on the rare examples of mankind, and, comparatively speaking, none too numerous beasts, that pass within his limited reach.

Often the men picked for my inspection masses of the gum seen exuding from the bark of many of the acacias. This remains ungathered in this district, partly owing to the depopulation of the country, and also to the competition of the superior article yielded in Kordofan, where it provides an emormous industry.

In so many tropical countries, subject to intense alternations between drought and wet, or more or less to drought only, it is noticeable how inadequate is the shade given by the trees. Scanty as is the provision of leaves, the Australian gum-trees (which do not seem to flourish in the Sudan) present their leaf-edges to the sun, and the hand of Nature seems turned against the animal kingdom. So in the Sudan, the shade cast by trees in general is of the most meagre quality.

One species of acacia, the talh, wears a strange aspect. In some localities it might be thought that industrious arboriculturists had taken extraordinary trouble and care to paint the trees from their base up to the topmost branching twig with a preparation of whitewash and sulphur, easily dislodged and staringly white. Such is the appearance of the bark, which annually peels, and the nearly leafless forests are weird where these warped and straggling trees abound. Another variety is, in as vivid a fashion, tinted an Indian red, and in many instances large globules of gum are seen exuding from the bark.

The stifling atmosphere as the wind dropped gave little incentive to move, even when the bank, a few hundred yards away, became alive with small, black, moving objects. The guinea-fowl were in thousands in their progress to the pools for their evening drink. These birds appear to be widely spread over Africa, and are equally numerous in the Northern Transvaal and Rhodesia. Wary and keen-sighted, they afford both sport and provision for the pot. The grilled breast of a young bird is by no means to be despised on the early morning trek. The leopard also takes his toll of their numbers, seizing them at night as they roost in the bushes.

In the early days of Rhodesia, when the memory of Lobengula still was fresh, travel was done in less luxurious fashion than in the Sudan of to-day—or, at least, in those parts where pack-animals can be employed. Long tramps with porters may be recalled, with a minimum of impedimenta; no camp-bed, no canvas bath, no cook or attendant, but merely the sheepskin kaross on the hard ground, the tins of bully beef, the billy and kettle for the provision of a hard-earned meal, and the rampart of baggage and thorns to give a semblance of protection in the darkness of the night.

Here the hot bath awaits one's return, the bath-room being bounded by a curtain hung up on one side, and the wide world on three others, a large grass mat serving as a carpet. In place of bully beef, or "road rations," stewed by oneself at the close of a tiring day, the dinner is ready to time, served on a white tablecloth. Use and custom are everything. In an incredibly short time after the end of a march, Abid would scrape a narrow hole in the ground, light a fire, and, placing two irons across it, prepare a meal, say, of soup, ariel tongue and onions, fillet of reed-buck, blanc-mange and prunes.

The failure so often is the bread, which the Arab insists on making with yeast, in tins and as heavy as lead, whereas in Rhodesia one made excellent loaves with the aid of baking-powder and an ant-hill oven, or "Kaffir pot," kept well covered with the dying embers of the sweet-smelling wood fire.

Wad Mustapha was a spot much looked forward to by my shikaris, eager, always eager as they were for meat. Sir Samuel Baker was once more brought to mind, for he wrote of the retreat of hippopotami from the Rahad to the Dinder. Here we were to find them; and on our way a reed-buck, one of the most graceful of the African antelopes, dashed lightly through the trees, and, stopping through a fatal curiosity to examine the intruders, paid its debt to Nature.

Far from the river-bank the camels halted, and careful advance was made to the fringe of bush, the luxuriance of which proclaimed once more the river, which our short cut had left to meander through miles of straggling curves. Elephant spoor was, as usual, in plenty, and any part of the thick, tangled scrub might have held one. Paths, irregular and many-branched, had been trodden into being by mighty feet, rendering progress easy; yet they were narrow, and breast-high grass concealed all else.

Far below, a careful glance revealed a still, deep pool, so large that neither end was visible, and stretching from bank to bank. Crocodiles lay stone-still on a sandy pit upstream; no ripple showed upon the water nor movement stirred the air. All was quiet; peace and rest was upon the world. Yet, as is so often the case in the affairs of man also, this tranquillity hid the whirlwind; the void in reality was full.

One feels virtue in the killing of the crocodile as of the snake, the enemies of all creation; and, with the wish to make atonement for the death of the inoffensive antelope, I moved gently forward to gain a position of vantage. What was the streak of ruddy light that burst noiselessly from the shade and concentrated quivering in the path ahead?

Crouched to the ground, tensely gathering its limbs beneath it, gripping the soil in purchase for its spring, a leopard faced me 50 yards away. Into so small a compass did he bestow his body that little but his head was visible, and an advance of a few yards was made before I knelt and fired. He shrank together once more; an instant elapsed before I could align my second barrel, and the magnificent, wicked beauty turned in a flash and leapt over the bordering grass, showing for a moment, broadside, all the rich colouring of his coat.

It is well to have a familiar in times of trial, however conscious one is of defects, to give assurance that it was not really one's fault, and the shikaris kindly, though quite incorrectly, suggested that a twig turned the ball. But a small piece of ruddy fur remaining on the ground showed how narrow was the escape.

It could not be expected that Mr. Crocodile would remain undisturbed by so unhallowed an interruption of his siesta, and his menacing snout was all that showed as he momentarily rose to investigate. So a shady bush was sought and an hour passed, while the sun mounted higher and higher. I fell to watching the multitude of birds arriving on fresh-burnt ground on the far side. The gravely deliberate marabout stork, with swallow-tail coat and bald head, seriously regarded the ground, as if with an interest scientific rather than predatory. Kites hovered incessantly over the flames, which crackled viciously in our ears, and dashed carelessly through the smoke on to some scorched mouse. Crows and cranes joined gaily in the sport, and the air was full of the burnt fragments of black ash.

In the midst of my lazy reverie, a breathing, bubbling sound burst oddly on my hearing, the water stirred, and a huge, black head rose from the depths of the pool beneath; cumbrously it turned and opened its jaws in a vast, phlegmatic yawn. Others became visible around it, and the hippo herd we had almost mourned as absent was before our eyes.

It is poor sport to shoot the beasts in water from the bank thus, and can only be justified by the desire for a specimen head, by their ravages in native crops, or by imperative need of meat for natives. Certainly an old bull is no mean antagonist; he will charge determinedly if he sees the opportunity, and is a desperate enemy to the small boats or canoes which may designedly or otherwise approach too near. But civilization is against him; the heavy rifle has robbed him of his chances, and he is disappearing, save in the trackless wastes of the marsh country and the remoter rivers.

The head of a hippopotamus is not quite the easy mark it might appear to be. As a rule, it is sunk low in the water, with the nostrils just above the surface, and the brain-box rises only 3 or 4 inches higher. At 100 yards distance it is therefore necessary to be tolerably accurate, for a bullet through any part but the brain would merely annoy him and cause a hasty retreat below the surface, whence he would return for an occasional breath and momentary glance to ascertain the position of affairs before diving into safety again.

My bullet found its way right up the snout, and he rolled about on the surface, mortally wounded, until a second shot pierced his brain, and he sank like a stone on the farther side.

The midday trudge three hours later over the hampering sand of the dry river-bed, rounding the far end of the pool, the stifling heat radiated by the elephant grass, which met well above our heads as we passed single file along tracks made by wild animals, must be experienced to be appreciated. Happy the black man, whose pigmented skin protects him partially from the effects of light and heat rays!

Forty yards away from the foot of the steep river-bank floated the great carcass, strangely little of it visible. To leave it longer would be to let it become the prey of the swarming crocodiles, whom my Arabs now prepared to dare. I took the pre-

RETRIEVING THE HIPPO.

NOOSING A WOUNDED HIPPO.

To face page 62.

caution of firing a few shots into the water to scare the reptiles, and with much shouting and splashing Fadl el Mullah swam out with a rope, a second man following. The society of the *timsagh*, as the Arabs name the crocodile, appeared to be an occasion of hilarious amusement; laughter and jests filled the air as the body rolled over on their mounting it.

Far away south in the "sudd" districts of the Mountain Nile, where the river sluggishly flows through interminable deserts of papyrus swamp, opening out here and there into wide lagoons, I had remarked the indifference of the Sudanese to the presence of crocodiles, and their cool behaviour under dangerous circumstances. On one occasion a scene took place which is exciting enough on the wounding of a hippo, when a man jumped overboard with a rope, and actually climbed on the animal to cast a noose over its head—succeeding eventually, after much dodging and struggle. Often, too, would the men engaged in cutting the channel clear of the vegetable growth carelessly swim from one sandal to another, thinking little of their rapacious enemies, the crocodiles and snakes.

On another occasion, on the same river, having shot a crocodile—whether killed or wounded I could not say—a huge negroid Arab, Sheikh by name, calmly skipped overboard into the shallow water and fished about with his feet, regardless of possibilities.

But thoughts are recalled to present events on

the Dinder; willing hands helped to pull the lassoed hippo ashore, and towed him a mile along the steep, shelving bank, and across the far end of the pool, to our camp.

Up the bank we, on the other hand, returned for the purpose of diving through the long grass we had passed through, and to search the country for other game. But the sight that met the eye was surprising. In the interval the whole landscape had undergone an almost theatrical "quick change."

For hundreds of acres, save for a belt through which we had passed when coming, in place of the rank, hay-coloured grass half smothering the stunted trees, the ground was bare and black, smouldering and smoking, little clouds rising from still live patches of fire. At the sides and extremities of the area, still extending to the river-bank, the vermilion flames leapt 30 feet into the air, running up the trees and devouring the dry creeping plants which enswathed them. For the time we were cut off from retreat, and nothing remained but to wait, sheltering from the heat, and to spend the time watching other hippos carefully rise to take stock of us, and the birds wheeling excitedly through the smoke cloud.

At one spot the flames died down for the moment; in another instant they might burst out again and rage at their fiercest. We sprang over the line of fire into the opening of a game track, and, with Gehenna now at our heels, walked smartly through the grass, turning a sharp corner—— Halt! Five yards away, the rest of the body hidden in a bush and grass, and quite invisible, were part of the hind-quarters of a huge, uncouth, recumbent animal, black-skinned and sparsely covered with short hair. A bull buffalo was resting in the heat of the day, and had passed along this track before us. No vital spot was visible, no approach from elsewhere showed itself; the cane-like grass stems gave scarce elbow-room on either side; with the fire behind us, it was backward or forward, with only a second's respite for choice of plans. I quietly retreated a few yards to a fork in the track, the men firing the grass, having no choice but to leave the buffalo to leeward as we went.

The ground was clear outside, and from a convenient point I awaited with my ·303 the on-rush of the flames and of a furious bull, left only 40 yards away.

The flames marched forward, and, drowned by their roaring crackle, one could hear no rustle of the grass; the patch was burnt out, and from our sad eyes the big black brute had vanished. I had trusted to the smoke from the fire of the grass masking our scent as we skirted round him, but he doubtless knew perfectly well each detail of our movements.

The sense of smell in this animal is developed to an extraordinary extent, and, combined with great cunning and savageness, probably justifies him in being classed one of the most dangerous of the

5

world's big game. It is stated that he has been known to double back parallel with his spoor in order to take his hunter in the rear as the latter followed the trail, and both he and the elephant are prone, more particularly when wounded, to indulge in a systematic search for their enemy, by circling to catch his wind.

The hide is exceedingly tough, and solid bullets are essential; cordite and nickel-cased bullets render *Bos Caffer* less formidable than in the days when Baker shot with black powder and a muzzle-loader, but in a buffalo killed on the White Nile one of my bullets was found hanging outside, with its nose just bedded in the hide.

There is an amount of uncertainty in the dispositions of buffalo, and the way they are likely to behave when approached by the hunter, which adds greatly to the interest of following them.

Some will bolt on the instant that their acute senses make them aware of danger; individuals may charge on sight, or the whole herd come down in a mighty rush. I remember, on one occasion, the crossing of a swamp, knee-deep and full of bent and tangled reeds and the pit-holes formed by hippo feet, with the herd I was stalking on the dry land just before me; I recall the eerie sensation that, should the herd employ concerted action, they would take seconds to cover that swamp where I could only painfully struggle along. But as the black heads turned to gaze at my companion and myself our rifles spoke; two wounded ones, hard hit, separated from the fleeting herd and awaited our oncoming. One charged determinedly with head outstretched as we drew close, but fell to a second shot before getting 10 yards nearer.

Natives are under very special restrictions in regard to the killing of game, but are necessarily exempted from punishment when they can show that they have acted in defence of their crops or their lives.

They may employ no firearm even if licensed to kill game, but subject to this may hunt any of the animals and birds which are not specially protected, as are the ostrich and others. On the other hand, a special licence may be granted which empowers them to kill these animals, a right which is denied the white man.

These limitations are in truth very liberal, and yet exceedingly necessary; otherwise it would be almost futile, in the preservation of game, to place restrictions on the comparatively small number of alien sportsmen, if hordes of natives with the increased facilities of the European had *carte blanche.* Naturally, in a vast area where officials are few, and many thousands of square miles have scarcely seen a white man, it is to be expected that complete enforcement of these regulations is by no means possible.

The cutting up of that hippo occupied the remaining hours of the day, and it was marvellous with what celerity the tough skin, an inch and a quarter thick, was taken off and cut into strips for converting eventually into the *kurbash*, or whip. I instructed the men to cut the head from the body for the purpose of preservation; so, in the characteristic native way of doing things backwards, they proceeded to cut the body off from the head by the simple means of dismantling the carcass and leaving the head until last.

This perverseness of the Arab or Berberi servant gives rise to sincere exasperation in torrid Africa; the following would constitute an adequate testimonial in the majority of instances:

"Mustapha has been on *safaria* with me for three months. His is a most excellent example of the well-known characteristics of the Berberi servant, and employers pleased with them will be delighted with Mustapha.

"He is quite strong, and too much work cannot be given him; in fact, the best way to keep him happy and contented is to give him a great deal to do, and to see that he does it. There is no need to talk gently to him; the most lurid command is obeyed with alacrity.

"While he has not yet the experience and knowledge of a highly trained European valet, from whose views and methods he would probably differ radically, he has learnt something from me, and has gratuitously received valuable advice from officers resident in the country as to his personal manners and conception of his duties.

"His knowledge of English is small, being confined to a few explicit words of which he has intelligently and quickly grasped the meaning. He will doubt-

THE HIPPO ASHORE.

READY TO BE CUT UP.

To face page 68.

less add to this knowledge with facility under future employers. He will before long attain a perfection which will prevent him from drawing corks with his teeth, offering the spout of the teapot rather than the handle, and a shirt inside out, and will refrain from the hitherto invariable practice of putting the wrong legging on the wrong leg. The complimentary term *Magnun* adequately describes him, and his greatest virtue lies in the fact that he does not snore, a valuable consideration when on *safaria.*"

But little of that hippopotamus was left for the crocodiles, hyænas, or leopards, that night; indeed, the utilization of nearly all parts, internal economy included, was an instruction to fastidious European taste. Strip by strip was cut away from the huge joints and hung on improvised rails well above the reach of four-footed marauders, to dry into biltong which would serve my camp-followers for weeks to come in their villages far behind.

By the evening of the next day the presence of the biltong had become impressive, but the Arab in these matters has no nose; neither camel nor semi-putrefaction are existent to him.

Many are the long walks undertaken, yielding all the incidents, or lack of them, which come to the fortune of a hunter. The shikari stops in his tracks and examines the ground, which may contain little, if any, meaning to an untrained eye; a whispered debate ensues, and while beaters make for one end of a narrow island in the dry river-bed, I make down wind to the other, and wait for flames to drive out the buffalo, whose tracks evidence his very recent presence and probable hiding-place. The notes of most hunters probably contain more records of game which they did not successfully stalk than of that brought back to camp; but in all sport the same story is told, and at the end of a season one feels that, after all, blanks and disappointments go to make keener the pleasurable recollection of rewards hard earned. So, if the buffalo did not appear, there was the joy of marking the clean leap of the reed-buck or oribi, the careful stroll of ariel or waterbuck feeding on the edges of *mayas* (swamps dried up at this season), the new spoor of elephant on grass-land burnt but yesterday, or the hyæna slinking away in the distance.

"Malesh" (Never mind) one mutters, and gravitates nearer to the peace of mind enjoyed by him who has secured all the trophies which his heart desires, in whom the instinct of the chase has died down, and who may await the appearance of wild creatures with the calm interest of a naturalist and student. Many a time and oft has the absence of a striking head of horns given me the opportunity of laying aside the rifle to give myself up to admiration of the "bonnie beasties" which it seems heartless to slay, here living, watchful ever, in the beauty of freedom.

The hippopotami deserted their pool that night. Their tracks were plainly visible in the black cotton soil, and were lost in the harder ground farther in the bush. Silently the lumbering animals had departed; the night had yielded no sound to us as we rested, and they had marched to some remembered spot where man was less likely to harass. Ereif el Dik, across a long neck of land round which the river had almost doubled on itself, had been scorned by them and left to the crocodiles. The latter are by no means easy to recover when shot. One hears the bullet strike the hard armour with a sounding whack, causing what are apparently lifeless tree-stumps to waken into astounding, slithering activity, fretting the water into muddy waves as they seek refuge, and leaving one, perhaps, shot through brain or neck, writhing in its last agony. But more often, if the bullet has not touched an instantly vital spot, the movement of the tail causes the animal to be caught by the slow river-current, or is sufficient to take it entirely into the water in which it already half lies.

Here the country is somewhat more undulating; no hills relieve the landscape, but occasional deep *khors* tell of swift-rushing torrents, adding fury to the summer flood. What now are eminences by the side of the river, with gullies to landward, high above river-bed, are islands or shoals later on. The rise of the water is amazing, and at Singa, where the banks vary from 50 to 70 feet above water in winter, it becomes necessary to use a felucca to traverse the lower part of the town area.

At these times travel, even on service, is impracticable, and mankind stops at home, mending leaky roofs as well as may be, while the wild beasts may be pitied! It is the elephant, judging from his tracks, who appears to feel least inconvenience, for the deep-sunk holes show that he wanders far and wide.

Fortunately for man and the softer-skinned animals, though the rain comes as a deluge, it does not last long at a time, and there are intervals of bright sunshine. The rank grass doubtless forms some kind of protection to such fragile creatures as oribi, but one would expect the wart-hogs to be drowned in the holes they find cover in during the winter.

The wart-hog is a common beast in many parts of the Sudan. Of ugly heads, his is the ugliest; dark slatey-brown in colour, he is disfigured by an excrescence on either cheek behind the curling, protruding tushes. Right in my path, from around a bush, one early morning came a great proud-looking beast, with his huge head and fore-quarters, proud-looking from the front, but shrinking into commonplace insignificance at the rear. When wounded, with all the obstinate pertinacity of the race, they are no mean antagonists, and their sharp tushes are formidable weapons. They do not appear to be excessively gifted with powers of sight, or else are too engrossed in thought to pay heed to external surroundings; for on occasion I have seen one unconsciously approach, and, waiting for him, have gently called, much to the amusement of my followers, "Ta allah hena" (Come here), until within easy shot. To my astonishment, they were readily taken as food by my Mahommedan companions, who on no account would touch my home-fed bacon, virtue apparently residing in the fact that the animals were wild, though I am not aware that the Prophet made any distinction in his injunction against the use of pig's-flesh. In the early days of the Transvaal, I recollect a very decided antipathy to the flesh of the native porker, owing even more to his indiscriminate appetite than to his leanness, for all was fish that came to his net, not excluding odd defunct Kaffirs.

On the far side, the direction for a time was between the Rahad and the Dinder. A waving sea of grass lay before us, through which we plunged for a mile or more, and which doubtless held much game. Countless buffalo might have rested in security in this *maya* without the slightest sign of their presence. In this uncertain possibility lies one of the charms of Africa. Any bush may hide a beast; a tuft of grass may give birth to sudden life; one's eyes become accustomed to an eternal roving yet unconscious watchfulness, and are ready to detect the slightest movement, unusual circumstance or form.

Moisture here shows its beneficent influence, for the other side of the *maya* (can this word be related to the corresponding "mere" in England?) is luxuriant in vegetation, being a trackless jungle of thick, branching trees with dense masses of creepers. Here our way had to be hacked out for us, and passage was difficult through entanglements of thorns and fallen branches. The mimosa thorns projecting from twin bulbous bases were of great size as compared with the starved product of the drier soil. The foliage was dry as tinder, and many ripened gourds of varied shapes hung from the vines; in the rich, moist warmth of the wet season the bush must present in itself a dense, impracticable obstacle.

Low-placed on a mule as I was, the passage was trying; the lower thorns caught one, but I ducked easily under the boughs. How then fared Abid the cook, perched high on his camel, dodging festoons of creepers, the spikes of mimosa, and branches which seemed to reach over to him with malicious intent, or the half-naked camel-drivers, whose skin seemed impervious to pricks, and the stumbles of their steeds of no consequence?

All rejoiced when the ground began to rise, miles later, and the bush thinned. As we emerged on the burnt-out forest we appeared to have driven game in front of us, for the first roan antelope (Abu Ooruf) we had seen evinced their acquaintance with our presence by moving off.

But we found our rejoicing premature; there came a dreadful trek across a breezeless, burning, shadeless furnace. It oppressed even the camelmen; the heat and glare struck us from the naked, blistering ground. The hardiest became quiet, all talking ceased; man and beast braced

HIPPO MEAT DRYING.

REED-BUCK AND WHITE-BARKED ACACIA.

To face page 74.

themselves stubbornly to endurance and dogged progression.

The Durraba Arabs who were good enough to accompany me for the sake of the meat I killed, and who doubtless acted in concert with the shikari, were quite disappointed that they were not provided with a hippo every day, and I noticed that the attention of all was fixed on *gamoos* (buffalo) in preference—indeed, until I realized it, almost to the exclusion of everything else. The most outlandish chance of finding buffalo was eagerly sought for, and various long walks indulged in after herds which had already sighted us and "vamosed." The hidden motive lay in the fact that the sooner donkeys could be loaded up with bales of dried meat, the less distance there would be for these worthies to travel back home. They, of course, constituted no tax on my caravan, but, on the other hand, refrained from being of any assistance unless actually obliged to, and were useless in the task of following up a wounded buck. Thereafter I trusted less to the judgment of my friend the shikari.

On a previous visit to the White Nile, it had been my misfortune to haunch a Mrs. Gray's waterbuck. For a couple of miles under the midday sun I followed it up, a sporting *bahari* (sailor) attending me to my undoing. Aware that in all likelihood it would lie down to ease its wound, I kept my eyes well open, and, seeing a crooked stick projecting from a clump of grass, cautiously approached, deeming it to be the horn of my quarry. Within 10 yards the intelligent native awoke to its presence, and gave notice of our arrival by calling to me in a hoarse whisper that this picturesque and by no means common antelope was in front of me. It took the hint, and, with the cleverness of most wild creatures, fled under cover of the high tussock of grass, and then in a direct line with the steamer, rendering it impossible to fire.

A further long chase ended in the imperative summons of the steamer's whistle recalling me, to my intense disgust and regret at having needlessly injured the poor creature. However, the glint of spears in the far distance told the story that the Shilluks were on its track, giving assurance that it would not be left to die from its wound or become the prey of lion or hyæna.

It was said that, when once on the track, the Shilluk will never leave such an animal, but will persistently walk it down. I have wished on various occasions for the presence of such determined sportsmen!

Evening was falling fast as Khor-el-Seneil was reached. Here was much marsh and water interpersed between the finest acacias which had yet been seen; the land was parklike and picturesque, with a sense of largeness and space, giving relief after the miles of consumptive-looking forest which lay behind. The cool of the evening and the drinking hour of game inspired new energy, accentuated by the discovery of an ariel which had fallen victim to a lion within recent days, and whose horns and scattered bones alone remained.

The sun descended and darkness fell before we located, as we thought, the position of our camp. The moon had not appeared; the ground was rough and broken; every few steps landed us in water or boggy land. The bush closed around us; thorn branches appeared endowed with malevolent life, and only silence met the calling of the men. It became obvious that we had badly missed our mark, and visions of a bedless night in the forest depths rose before us. But a distant song broke in on our lucubrations—a familiar rhythm which oft in the stilly night had wakened sleepers and attracted carnivora. The senseless advertisement that here in the flesh, and blind in the darkness, was the favourite food of lions, in this instance proved our guide, and slowly we stumbled onward, guided by the hideous braying of Ibrahim's ass.

Truly, the light-built Arab is not such a trial to his steed as is the European of stouter build. But the wide cracks in the soil and its unstable character might be thought sufficiently onerous under even a light-weight. Yet the donkey, with unshod feet, still plugged easily along when Ibrahim mounted without halting, merely placing his right foot on the donkey's neck and shunting himself lightly back into position.

Wad-el-Hag is a relic of bygone days. Now merely a name, it was the site of the farthest up-river permanent village in the days before the Mahdi rose.

A sardine tin, left by some sportsman and picked clean by the ants, is the sign that the hunter is now its only visitor.

Ibrahim was in the Abu Hashim district as a young man in those days—after all, but a few short years ago—and significantly draws his hand across his throat, purses his mouth, shakes his head, and says much in Arabic; for in this district, now almost deserted, were once 800 villages. Yet many there were who spoke well of Mohammed Ahmed, the Mahdi, remembering him by his early affectation of piety, his magnetic personality, his pretence of asceticism and imposition of virtue on others, rather than by his rapacity, bloodthirstiness, and immorality. There was a belief in his *bona fides* which caused them to overlook the terrible results of his rule, but for Abdulla, the Khalifa, his successor, no word of good was said, save in reference to his soldiership and pluck.

Day by day fresh sights were afforded; at one moment the eye was struck by an odd, scrambling, most un-antelope-like movement through the trees. It was the crablike retreat of the great ape, keen-eyed and vengeful; even the Arabs discountenance the killing of one of a troop, in the belief that his fellows in retort will attack in menacing combination. In the *gebels* (hills) are also many baboons, and it is said in South Africa of these, that one of their great aims in fighting is to bite off their opponent's fingers. Truly, an ape without fingers would cut a poor figure in a tree, and it demonstrates an exact appreciation of adapted strategy.

Far away, too, in the wilderness of thorn scrub was a slanting patch of brown, crowned by two small prominences visible against the skyline as they topped the trees. The glass revealed a living animal of large dimensions, chestnut in its figured markings, dainty and supercilious in every movement and expression.

The giraffe in these qualities brings to one's mind the high-bred, supersensitive and ultra-refined maiden lady of mellow age, to whom the propinquity of the world is a desecration, whom the touch of a flower would almost defile, and who lives in a perpetual detachment of self from aught that approaches the common conditions of life.

Keen vision is the defence of the giraffe, aided by the eminence from which he views the neighbourhood; but if one of those great legs came into play with a well-planted blow, naught else would be required to silence even the stoutest of enemies.

As I cautiously approached under cover of a bush, he ceased browsing on the topmost leaves of the mimosa, and it was only by spreading wide his immense front-legs that even his lengthy neck enabled him to pluck the grass beneath him.

At various times I have found the bones of this timid and harmless animal bleaching in the sun, showing that the lion had evaded his telescopic sight, and had struck him unawares, perhaps at night. But now he was on the *qui vive*, and full

300 yards still separated us when he quickly erected his legs to the perpendicular, stared an instant, and with a mate went off in the queer lurching fashion caused by both legs on the same side being advanced together.

The hide is esteemed by the natives for making sandals ; and part of the bone of the front-legs, almost ivory-like in appearance, is sharpened and employed by one tribe—I believe the Anuaks, on the Sobat—as a spear-head. But to the European it would seem a tragedy to lay this beautiful creature low, harmless as it is, and doomed to extinction except under laws of strict preservation.

It was some days later that, undesirous of killing, I expressed my desire to photograph one from close quarters. At Beit-el-Wahash the opportunity arose. An uninteresting walk with little incident had nearly come to a close, when the word "Zeraf" was whispered.

Rifle was left behind, and the camera substituted. Every bush, tussock of grass, and undulation, was taken advantage of, and still the great fellow unconcernedly plucked the tree-tops. Ibrahim stayed behind one bush while I crawled forward on my stomach under cover of another. Arriving within 40 yards of the great bull, standing broadside on, he presented so enormous an appearance that I wondered if the picture would actually include the whole animal. I was surprised also at the vividness of his colouring against the thin grey trunks of the trees, for so much has been said of the value of his protective colouring, which is no doubt assisted by the patchwork character of his marking.

I became aware of another long neck beyond, looking over a ridge of bush directly at me. It was of a sober brown in colour instead of chestnut, and had hitherto been unobserved. Realizing that my chance was passing, though the bull was still too much absorbed in the aerial foliage to dream of creeping things upon the earth (an idea of one's personality which had not before presented itself), I bent my head to the view-finder, pressing the button, and looking up found not two, but four, giraffes in full, lumbering flight.

On development of the photograph, it was astonishing to note how—in the absence of the contrast between the colours of hide and tree-trunks—the lanky proportions of the animal merged into the other components of the landscape; so much so was this that, aided by the fact that exposure was made at the instant he discovered my presence at short range and was bounding round just facing me, it was actually difficult to outline him.

Lions appeared to be plentiful here, their tracks being quite fresh, and at Ein-el-Shems, where we had rested a day or two previously, camp had been pitched in the sand of the river-bed, not far from a pool, whence next morning was seen the trail made by enterprising crocodiles. This night the asses were particularly persistent in their braying: was it a note of defiance? for the morning showed—200 yards away on the farther shore—the fresh spoor of four lions, two large and two small, who had apparently been inspecting us from afar as we slept.

Leaving the camels to follow, we plough patiently up the weary river-bed, and often see a wee speck on the distant sand, which we feel sure is looking at us—mere sensation, but still distinct. As we march it expands, and a point sticks out at one side. This point develops two further ones above, and the speck becomes a watchful buck with head and ears defined. Often it does not move until 500 yards divide us, when it airily skips over the soft, deep sand which causes our animals such trouble and toil.

The lion had been more or less of a shadow and a fantasy since my departure, but now for the first time we heard him, far behind us in the distance. No fewer than six had been shot here by a party which passed us, perhaps accounting for the respectful distance from which this animal spoke. A great growling grunt boomed through the atmosphere as the sun sank low, and was repeated continually with decreasing intervals; then silence, and the cadence began over again.

The oncoming darkness augmented the impressiveness of the sound, and the shikaris, recognizing the futility of a chase, fell to mimicking the mannerisms of his tones with hilarious amusement; but those whose life is not cast continually amongst wild beasts can but feel instinctively that the animal is surely great which can impress the world so deeply merely with the vastness of his voice. A shadowy reed-buck flitted from the bank; the spoor of a yesterday's elephant was passed—that great flat pad which expresses so much; and in the darkness the isolated police post near the Khor Galegu was reached, amid the excitement of its solitary occupants.

The baggage camels were late in arrival, and I wondered how the servants liked the monarch's voice. I asked Abid if the lion talked to him; grinning, he replied, "Yes, sir, he talk very big too much." Then followed the usual vocal illustration. But silence had come with the darkness; Arab conversation is not usually quiet, less quiet amongst the camel-men this evening, perhaps, because the guns had been far ahead, and their voices were doubtless wafted down to the owner of the deep bass voice, which forthwith was still.

Yet can he in justice claim the title "King of Beasts"? His courage when at bay—great as it is—is no greater than that of the buffalo, and his methods are those of the sneak and the footpad. Cunning, as a rule, is his controlling influence rather than a broad intelligence, and even his loose-limbed majesty of stride fails to enthrone him.

He must yield the sceptre to the elephant, who by reason of courage, size, strength, and intelligence, surpasses all other animals. In how few creatures of the brute creation exists any germ of true unselfishness! Thought for others of the species, save in the deep-implanted instinct maternal, or the loneliness on the death of a mate, again egotistic, is rarely in evidence. Even man's best friend, the dog, would pass a wounded brother with a sniff; if wild, he would probably devour him.

The noblest impulse of mankind is to care for the unfortunate, to succour the disabled. Who that has seen a wounded elephant rescued from danger by his fellows, supported on either side, can deny in this an attribute superior to every other?

It is tempting, too, to accuse him of possessing a bump of humour. A train of donkeys once fell foul of a herd. Attention was concentrated on the loads they carried. With all the mischief of monkeys, these were torn asunder, their contents being distributed over half the province. Rumour had it that beer-bottles were found with their corks drawn, but this is believed to be either a libel or due to the expansive effect of the heat.

At Bor, on the Mountain Nile, they were at one time full of practical jokes. Passing at night-time through the village, they would knock the sleepers up by demolishing their huts above their heads, then contentedly march away.

They deem it excellent sport, too, to stroll about a native garden. Their deep-sunk footprints will make good reservoirs after the rains, and to pluck the dhurra plants by the roots is commendable in view of its educational effects. The African human is lazy and should be made to work, and he

JUNCTION OF THE KHOR GALEGU WITH THE DINDER.

CAMP ON THE DINDER.

To face page 84.

certainly will require to do so at the conclusion of these perambulations. Thoughtfulness for others in this case is ironical; too often it is much misplaced, for many a crop is all that stands between the life and semi-starvation of the unhappy owner.

A picture rises before me of a bizarre, naked figure in the grass of the river-side of the same district, violently bending and straightening his knees, and shaking his outstretched hands and arms, during the time my boat remained in sight. It was designed to ward off the "evil eye" which might be cast upon his crops, causing their destruction by disease or marauders.

Small wonder his concern; that evening a bull elephant was wounded just before my arrival. Night fell, and in the early morning we started on the trail, wading the black water of the *khor*. The numbers of the herd were very great, and a square mile of country was covered with fresh evidences of their presence. There were piles of steaming dung, some trees broken short off, others simply uprooted, but no elephant remained. The wounded one had no doubt been helped away, and the easy six-mile-an-hour saunter had taken them far inland before we appeared on the scene.

Here on the ground was a fragment of white ivory, broken from the tusk of some cow as she uplifted a tree-root. Almost invariably one tusk is used in preference, showing in consequence unequal wear; and she would now be thrown on to the use of the unbroken one. In some cases the placing of the tusk under tree-roots causes a notch to be eventually worn an inch or so from the extremity.

Two or three days would probably elapse before they came near the place again—indeed, it was probable that they would leave it severely alone; so, after many miles' walk in the hope of coming up with them, pursuit was abandoned.

The sergeant (*umbasha*) of police and his three or four men at Khor Galegu led, with the Sheikh of Galegu, solitary lives indeed. Their days were gladdened by two Hebes of dilapidated aspect, who must have been banished from the home community for their looks. A few reed huts sufficed for their protection from sun and beast; the *angaribs*, clay water-pots, and gourds, their household goods. Below was the patch of ground where grew a small supply of dhurra and the coarse melon which delights the native heart, and by the river-bed was the thick-foliaged and imposing tamarind-tree, which afforded shade and medicine, and provided a lookout post into the bargain.

Seventy miles or so from Singa, it constitutes the last post on the Dinder, save the slavery post at Abu Ramleh, on the Abyssinian frontier. Eastward runs the Galegu through desolate country, far into the hills of Abyssinia, enclosing with the Dinder to the south a land unmapped, unknown, save to the few natives who guard too well the secret of the water-holes.

During the dry season these men remain here as

a sign of authority, and doubtless to keep watch on any intruding Abyssinians, so the advent of a sportsman is a welcome event to break the monotony of their lives.

A teacupful of honey was hospitably provided, and a gourdful of liquor with honey as its base; it was sickly and probably slightly intoxicating, and my powers of drinking the beverage were viewed with contempt.

CHAPTER V

WILD LIFE AMONGST BEASTIES

In the Sudan, as in Rhodesia, the honey-indicator exercises its profession of utilizing mankind for the exploitation of a previously acquired knowledge of a bees' nest. Community of interest is not often found between birds and men, and that this community should be initiated by the bird is strange indeed. The elephant or buffalo hunter knows to his cost the perfect understanding between the giant and his white-feathered companion, who, sitting on his back, keeps one eye on the ticks that infest his host, and an equally sharp one on any unfriendly approach.

But the action of the honey-guide goes a step farther; its motive is not merely to give passive warning, but is an active request and inducement to a human being to perform a certain specific deed —to follow its direction and take the honey it has discovered.

No one can sit in camp in the daylight without being struck by the daring of the kites or buzzards. They will dash in amongst one's belongings, snatching at any scrap of food, and whirling away again to circle round, watching with keen vision for a further opportunity.

Vultures sit around sullenly expecting the shifting of the camp, waiting to chime in with the others, but rejecting that which the buzzards—foul feeders as they are—consume. The omnipresent and cheerful crow keeps industriously on the move, and his neat appearance when at rest contrasts pleasantly with the ragged, dirty aspect of the buzzard.

The site of a camp recently moved is a lesson in scavenging: buzzards and vultures crowd the ground in all postures; the marabout, called Abu Sin ("father of teeth"), from his immense bill, joins in the quest while minutiæ of crumbs and the savoury skimmings of meat tins go to the share of numberless ants.

One day three hartebeest, hitherto unseen, dashed from behind a clump and galloped away, carrying their narrow, long-drawn-out heads high in the air. Roan antelopes appeared midst the trees, and through the grass I distinguished the great forms, as bulky as that of a horse, with thick necks and stout, back-curved horns. Between us were some reed-buck which proved my undoing. So successful a stalk was made on hands and knees that I arrived within 20 yards of these fawn-coloured creatures, and marked the quick movements of the male. Progress was useless; the reed-buck caught our wind, I saw his lips lift up as he gave a shrill cry, and away the herd bounded toward the roan, sending them onwards.

"Bashmak batal, ibn el kelb," swore Ibrahim, demonstrating the Oriental contempt for the friend of man—"Reed-buck bad, son of a dog"; but it is all part of the sport—a part which Ibrahim, keen only on getting meat, could not comprehend. To the Arab there appears no pleasure in the study of wild life; Nature does not appeal to him save in rare instances; the quick start, the frightened attitude and expression, the warning note, of the reed-buck conveyed no sense of beauty, commanded no admiration.

Appreciation of aggressive qualities of course there is; the power of the lion, the courage and sagacity of the buffalo and elephant, appeal to man's emulation and sense of self-protection, but the gentleness and timidity of the harmless gazelle inspires no corresponding feeling.

The Sheikh of Galegu had overtaken us, probably with a view to obtaining gifts of unconsidered trifles. He had brought for my acceptance a small duck egg, which, proving to be minus the usual infantile duckling, was, in spite of its insufficiency, a gift indeed. His happiness was exuberant on receiving in return two fishhooks, a few cigarettes, and the skin of a tiang. These people are crude enough, but he was exceedingly polite, expressed his pleasure at having seen me and his gratitude for my gifts; he at least knew the formulæ of social usage, and I could not help wondering if he had learnt to use them as superficially as so many of his European cousins. He had come in late in the evening with a spear and only one eye. What comfort there is in accustomedness! The white man is foolish and always on his guard, so to speak; his eyes rove from bush to bush with expectation, and he feels the moral support of a ·400 rifle. These are black men who dare the paths of leopard and lion with merely a piece of sharpened iron on the end of a stick—yet command their respect. The recent footprint of a lion at large on his native soil affords a sensation to a frequenter of Regent's Park which is mere amusement to the man who is born amongst four-footed enemies; yet their hate is stronger than ours for the great cat, and their delight at his fall more full of enthusiasm.

The diary is written in the midst of great darkness; "Mrs. Sun"—as I have to call the moon in my ignorance of the Arabic term—just having been born, knowledge of the world around is bounded by the narrowest limits. The night air is dry and warm, tempered by a cool breeze. Talk about Robin Hood and the greenwood tree, he must have had rheumatism! The grey tree skeletons vacillate in the flicker of the fires. No landlady's coal-scuttle feeds our flames; whole trees burn to give warning to lion that they had best seek other meat than man, camel or donkey (to say nothing of my mule and the hippo meat). No "shilling a night" oil-lamp shows up the sphinx-like shape of the camel, grotesque and motionless, and the kindly black forms crouching round, full of response to a cheerful song. It is the firelight of the forest, the resource of primeval man, the guardian of the camp, the terror of the great growler who made the heavens reverberate in the evening.

The contrast with the animals of the camp becomes the greater; one contemplates the little goat that nestles down at one's feet, or by a case of Piper Heidsieck, as sweetly as if it knew no other home—the advertising and useful ass who hee-haws to the croaking of the frogs—the (thank God) sometimes silent camel, who, were he more noisy, could scarcely be forgiven his stink—the cricket sounding just the same as on one's grandfather's hearth: all so happy in their association, and homely by contrast with the great man-eating beasts which wait outside the charmed circle.

It being some years since I found myself in a Zoological Gardens with all the beasts let loose, where man is only a sample of one of God's creations turned out amongst many other varieties, it is not to be wondered at that sometimes sleep does not come too early, and that then it is liable to be broken.

Last night it was the gentleman whose finger-print had been taken on the soft cotton soil who evinced from a short distance his fondness for our society. He made remarks to us, probably insulting, at short intervals all through the night, from various positions in regard to the camp. This is where the unaccustomed European, used to being shut up in a safe cage all night, feels foolish. He *hears* his black brethren sleep soundly, observes the perfect insouciance of camels and donkeys, yet he is stupid enough to feel glad when the fires are bright, and sorry when they are dull, and he follows the movements of *Felis leo* by his voice from place to place with animated and quite unnecessary interest.

Each remark consisted of from twenty to twenty-four words, the early ones sounding a distinct tone of complaint, declining on two notes and staccato in the finish; the later ones had less of an interval between them, and were of one gruff note only, subsiding at the last into a heavy sigh or breath.

"Ah," said Abid next morning, "he tell his wife his stomach full, he *mabsoud* [happy]. If he hungry he no say anyting."

He failed to respond, however, to the strictest search when the daylight came, and may have passed on to join his comrades down-river.

It was strange, on the other hand, that, though night after night the camping-places were haunted in this way, on no single occasion on this river did I fall across one in the daylight, during the scores of miles of every class of country we traversed.

Among the Arabs who followed me for the sake of the meat, now presenting a formidable appearance, was a whilom slave of the notorious Zobeir Pasha, whose influence extended far into the interior of slave-raided Central Africa, and whose services Gordon desired to enlist to preserve Khartoum.

My friend was possessed of a large, round, clean-shaven headpiece, and was quite a pantomime artist.

He felt dissatisfied with an insufficiency of meat according to his high ideals, so with a noble grin picked up a resounding, hollow gourd, tapped it first, and then his stomach. This, in spite of a ton or more of hippo and a number of buck.

So one morning Ibrahim and he went out to prospect; I was seedy, and glad to delegate some of the search. Ibrahim returned crestfallen, poor fellow, and had to make up with a fib (he had probably found honey and rested under a tree most of the time). So he reported that he had done great things; that he had discovered an elephant lying asleep, but, of course, it was useless to come back to me, as I was not shooting them on the Blue Nile.

The comedian bore out his statement with much profusion of gesture and language, so I asked him to bring the elephant here, when I would provide him with plenty of meat, for which he had been offering a very long prayer to Allah on behalf of his children. His answer was obvious, and was accompanied by a smile which evinced recognition that the story had failed, and gave the show completely away.

Nevertheless, having perhaps observed my partiality for eggs in the matter of the Sheikh of Galegu, with much ado he produced no fewer than three. He was evidently a wit of the very first order and qualified for a native music-hall, for the eggs were the size of wrens', and, indeed, were already inhabited.

Not that the Sudanese fowls, being of the ordinary African type, can claim an enormous advantage over the wren in point of weight. Dry of flesh, too, and scraggy of body, they are invariably tough as rhinoceros hide, partly owing to the habit of killing them just before meal-time.

A startling agility is exhibited when they are chased, and at Singa I once witnessed a ridiculous sight. Two ancient and skinny greybeards, their few rags flying behind in the breeze, coursed full tilt across the square at top speed, spears in hand but reversed, in the wake of a nimble but very small fowl. The fowl doubled smartly, and "Father Abraham," following suit, missed his footing and rolled head over heels in the dust. All the dignity remained with the chicken, which flew to a roof-top and justifiably crowed!

Piggy was out for an airing one day, and strolled along in his usual casual fashion. He unfortunately took too long in investigating me, and fell a victim, owing to fresh meat being wanted for the men. It gave an opportunity of witnessing the terrible destructive effects of the expanding ·400 bullet. I wounded him badly at first, but had to take a flying shot as he went off, to stop him. The bullet, coming from behind, completely destroyed one hind-quarter, causing a rent a foot long, and blowing a large piece out at the exit.

Wakening from a siesta in late middle day, when nearly all creatures indulge in like fashion, I saw a small animal 20 feet above my head, lying curled up round an uncomfortable twig. It proved to be a genet cat taking a rest, opening her eyes occasionally, but taking no notice of proceedings underneath. These little things feed on birds and small animals, and are quite as much at home amongst the twigs as the former. It is rather unfair to the small bird or animal that there should exist no night refuge whatever where sleep may be without danger, that no hour of the twenty-four should be free from the fear of a painful death. So I felt mean to take advantage of her innocence or trust, and took care that she dropped dead without knowledge of danger or pain.

Dull yellow in colour, with brown spots, a long, ferret-like head, and a prehensile tail as long as the body, the genet is a member of the civet family, but differs from them, inasmuch as its claws can be completely retracted, and the slit of the eye is vertical.

I often noticed that the boys were fond of picking certain solitary sticks of grass, and they once drew my attention to the smell of a substance adhering to them, which excited my abomination rather than pleasure. They informed me that it was much in request by their sweethearts, who regarded it as a precious perfume. The ladies of the Sudan became even less perfect in my eyes on hearing this. The practice of fumigating themselves with the sweet-smelling smoke of such woods as sandal or talh has a much more useful effect, as it replaces the characteristic odour of the African human with that of a vegetable.

The gummy material on the grass-stems, so coveted by Arab beauty, and gathered little by little into quills as we progressed, was in fact deposited by the civet-cat, and my strictures on the taste in native perfumery in this country must be modified by the fact that the musk when properly treated, combined with other substances—and, I should say, vastly diluted—is used as a base in Europe for many varieties of scent.

My friend of the empty stomach had the laugh over me one day—mirth joined in by his fellows. Flitting in the alternate shade and sunlight of the trees, I saw a bird with golden wings, and flight erratic as that of a snipe. I coveted it as a specimen — not to eat, as the clown naturally thought—and after much trouble fired, and it fell. A long search ended by the discovery of a *bat*, whose wings were transparent yellow in the sunshine. Big-game shooting is not supposed to include such small deer as this, and when the boys saw my disappointed face, and that I proposed neither to eat nor to skin it, I was thought a fit subject for quite respectful amusement.

It is well that the number of reed-buck which may be shot in one season is limited, for their flesh, being very passable eating, renders them preferable as fresh meat. Waterbuck is quite impossible to the European, being rank in flavour, though the natives find no disadvantage in the fact. And how welcome fresh meat is after the continued meals emerging from tins laboriously brought from Chicago or France!

I have often imagined the expression of an English cook were she asked to produce dishes of equal excellence to those of Abid, with a kitchen range of such simplicity as his. True, he made an occasional mistake, as when he served a whole tin of "pâté de foie gras" *hot* and oily! But he made up for such lapses by his application in catching fish in the pools, where the fickle river had crowded them. The crocodile is mainly a fish-eater; thousands of cranes and storks tread the shallows; fish-eagles and kingfishers dart into the depths; and the marvel is that, even in their initial multitudes, a single fish remains in each circumscribed home to see the first flush of summer torrents from the hills.

The fish which he succeeded in taking did not equal in flavour the Dover sole. Its appearance was that of a mustachioed dogfish, black in colour, on whose enormous head an elephant had placed its foot. The body constituted only one-half of its length, and was built vertically; while the evil-looking head, fringed round the mouth with eight fleshy tentacles, was flat. Others, which were entirely uneatable, and also tentacled, almost resembled the eel, with a dorsal fin the whole length of the body.

It is said that some classes of fish—though I saw

none—live in mud cracks when the river falls, developing lungs in place of gills for the time being.

Water, often very muddy, taken from pools so crowded with life is not fascinating, and it was generally obtained by sinking a hole in the river-sand, which has thus filtered it to some extent. But none was good enough to dispense with boiling or the Pasteur filter, which only severe measures induced my attendants to employ for me invariably.

By this time we had penetrated well into the loveliest country of the Dinder. Singa lay far behind to the north-west; Khartoum beyond it, remote as a distant dream; Kassala, some hundreds of miles north-east, with Gedaref, fertile and prosperous before the blight of the Mahdi fell on it, watched the same Abyssinian barrier, which will soon turn us westward to rejoin the great central waterway of the Sudan. Meanwhile the lack of human society was compensated for by that of beasties and birds.

I had sent Sheikh Ali of the camels back for more animals, the heads having become rather too numerous for my carrying power, and one camel having fallen sick.

On his return, I inquired, with some anxiety, after the Sheikh of Durraba, whom I had doctored unwittingly in so heroic a fashion. I was relieved to find that I had not killed him, as I feared, but that a complete cure had been effected, much to the enhancement of my reputation. Shereef, a second shikari who had accompanied me from Durraba, had also prayed for medicine for his wife; but, not having investigated "Sitt" (Mrs.) Shereef's case personally, owing to motives of delicacy, I regret to say I had made no impression on her case with sundry "Livingstone Rousers." Unfortunately, the lady became so ill that Shereef, who was a very keen sportsman and intelligent ex-member of the police, had to leave me.

It is quite amusing what faith these people have in one's healing powers—a faith justified more by the effect of Epsom salts or calomel than by powers of diagnosis. The impression is arrived at inevitably that they like being doctored, and Sheikh Ali immediately informed me that the sun had hit him in the back, for which he required medicine. As a matter of fact, he was stiff with hard riding, so hot water and "Elliman" were prescribed, and I saw that the latter was not taken internally!

Some ten miles' journey in the early morning brought us opposite to the Khor Semsir, where we found ourselves at the edge of a very extensive *maya* with a low knoll here and there, and patches of rough grass dotted over the plain.

A wart-hog sneaked away as we reconnoitred, and a few gazelle grazing on the edge bounded away into the thicket, but far in the middle was a scattered herd of the Tora hartebeest. Leaving a man with instructions to show himself in half an hour's time, we made a long détour, and, striking the *maya* at the far side, came unexpectedly within 300 yards of a bull. The *maya* was so open that it seemed impossible to approach very near, and the only cover was provided first by a thin bush, and then by an ant-hill about 200 yards away. Crawling on one's stomach is not the pleasantest of operations even on English turf, but here, under the fierce sun, with short grass-stems damaging the palms of the hands, with the ash of burnt grass flying into one's nostrils, and perspiration streaming into the eyes, the pursuit of pleasure is tinged with pain. By the time the ant-hill was reached, the hartebeest had become aware of something unusual, and, apparently not being gifted with the highest intelligence amongst beasts, was standing almost directly facing me. I decided to risk the shot, and, somewhat to my modest surprise, he fell motionless, the bullet having pierced the base of the neck and the main arteries of the heart.

One does not always profit by previous experience, and that morning I had neglected to bring a pair of gloves which I usually carried. The Arabs objected to my white face and hands, saying that they frightened the game. Later in my journey they inspired the lords—or rather ladies—of creation with similar terror.

The hands one could cover with dark gloves, and keep studiously still when stalking—a simple enough precaution, but less easy to continue than one would think. The white face, however, even though tanned and shaded by the big *burneto*, or pith helmet, must show plainly in the brilliant sunlight, and an occasional glint of the sun on the spectacles betrays the presence of a moving object to the game.

A difficulty with one's Arabs at first lies in enforcing silence after a kill; many a time it is possible to find game within a reasonable distance even after the noise of two or three shots, but, unless sharply forbidden, the sight of meat lying at their feet appears too much for their feelings.

Later in the afternoon I saw a herd of roan antelope moving slowly to the bush at the far side of the *maya*.

It became a matter of doubt who would reach the point first; I, with the disadvantage of being half a mile behind them, having to make a long half-circle in the bush, cautiously and quietly.

Anxiously I peered through the openings, finding the herd still moving steadily on, and now abreast of my position, a neck-and-neck race. Back into the bush again, but some eddy of wind had told them of danger, and, slightly hastening their pace, they streamed into the forest 200 yards ahead of me, their lumbering gallop taking them quickly through the trees and out of view.

I saw few snakes in this country, but on our return journey, with a second hartebeest, my men gave a sudden cry, and a few yards ahead a large snake darted away to its hole, wherein a portion of its body was visible.

Vituperation filled the air, and perhaps it was well that no literal meaning was conveyed to my mind. They stated it was poisonous, but natives so seldom discriminate between these and harmless ones that it was by no means unquestionable.

Some days are, naturally, barren in results save in pleasure—the pleasure of stalking and attaining close proximity to herds of antelope without the wish to interfere with them, as they feed unsuspiciously near.

In the evening comes the amusement of shooting guinea-fowl for the making of soup or as provision for breakfast. On occasion one of the Berberi servants would be detailed to obtain them, and it became an unbroken practice, on return to camp, to ask, "Mustapha, fi gedad?" (Are there guinea-fowl?) with the almost invariable answer, "Ma fisch" (There are none), and a lengthy explanation that they would not wait for him to fire. The desire of an Englishman to shoot birds flying is incomprehensible to them—it is so much easier to kill a bird when it is standing still on the ground; but they are lost in admiration when birds fall dead in mid-flight.

One night the question "Fi gedad?" failed to produce a smile on Mustapha's face. He rolled himself up in a blanket, and felt as helpless as a sea-sick lady in mid-Channel. Even the lion which talked to us that night failed to make Mustapha lie nearer the fire; in fact, it is doubtful whether the idea of transmutation of Mustapha into lion troubled him much. Malaria made him green and sickly, and he put himself under my care with all the abandon of an infant.

No longer was my water-bottle mouth cleaned with his finger, or the tumblers washed in dirty water, when I was not looking. He was relieved from the daily cleaning of my boots, which was such useless trouble, as they only got dirty again. The night-drink, so carefully placed just out of my reach, was attended to by others, and the demonstration of the way how *not* to do things was for the time suspended.

So I mixed him a drink made of the cream of tartar surrounding the pips of the tebeldi-tree fruit, which bears the same reputation as a febrifuge here as it does in South Africa. In this he had marvellous faith, and alternated it with quinine. I noted, on recovery, that he credited the native medicine rather than the quinine with his restoration to health.

An advantage of the Dinder at this season is the absence of mosquitoes, and it is only the attention of flying bugs of sorts which render the use of nets advisable.

A few miles onward, our camels lagging a mile or so behind us, we crossed a *maya* into the scrub beyond, and as we did so two great slanting necks appeared a few hundred yards away. The angle which a giraffe's neck makes with the line of ground-level is a peculiar one, and causes the appearance of an eternal yearning after something that cannot be reached, and which is invisible to the observer. In this instance, after a few moments' cropping of the grass with their legs wide spread, they spotted the camels in the distance, and departed, leaving a tiny imprint in a photographic film.

The bank of the river, explored by Ibrahim and me, was fringed with thick, creeper-covered jungle, of a denser character than usual. The grass was high and rank, and made the paths of hippo, buffalo, and elephant, the only possible ways for us to take.

A rustling in the grass made us stop suddenly; something had seen or winded us—perhaps had been waiting our approach—and had moved on. But not for many yards. We progressed carefully, with eyes all round us, and nerves collected and tense. I saw small monkeys in a tree 20 yards away, a bank of grass intervening, excitedly moving and chattering, giving news of some enemy's proximity. A step onward, and then, with the agility and power which is so amazing, a splendid leopard bounded into the path ahead.

I wished to make no mistake this time, and advanced so as to get a clear view and sure aim at a much shorter distance. But "Nimr" saw the rifle, and would not wait. I felt somewhat akin to Mustapha and his *gedad,* for the leopard leapt back into the darkness of a tree, and doubtless escaped down a deep ditch close by, for no more was seen of him. It appeared to me that he was of a yellower colour than the previous one, which was ruddy and ringed, but the shade made it difficult to judge.

Here we pitched our camp, as the ground was high, and shaded by two fine tamarind-trees (ardeb). Mustapha, still incapacitated by fever, was given a drink composed of a decoction of the fruit, and retired to a broken rest; and the full moon, here almost directly overhead, soon looked down on men snoring, chattering, praying, or singing, while the camels chewed aloud and the donkeys bellowed.

It is strange in what light esteem woman is held by the Arab. A beast of burden, a slave without a soul, she has no hope of reaching Paradise, though, to the Arab, Paradise without woman one would have thought impossible. She ministers to his wants and prepares his food, but she is of so small account that daughters are not reckoned as children, and in inquiring how many children there are in a family, the question is, "How many *boys* have you?" Yet I imagine that here, as elsewhere, feminine influence is a power not underrated by wise men.

The ever-ready Fadl el Mullah, always so fond of a joke, was delighted at being styled "the white," as he plastered his thick-lipped mouth with the dry white powder of the tebeldi fruit, and repaid me by lighting a smoky fire of the perfumed talh wood between me and the camels. He inquired how many sons I had, and endeavoured to please me by ofttime repeating the name of my schoolboy son, saying: "Basil Effendi will come to the Sudan;

Ibrahim will guide him to shoot his first lion; Fadl el Mullah will skin it; Bachit Abdullah will carry his water-bottle and lead his mule; while Abdullah the father will guard the camp and make a good shade for the *angerib*." Always, when things had gone wrong and a shade appeared over my face, these good fellows would think to lift it by firstly a whispered "Basil Effendi!" one to the other, rising to full tones, and a smile when they saw it had caught my ear.

This sense of duty on the part of the Arab guide had its counterpart in that of the native of the Hebrides, who, acutely conscious of Dr. Johnson's expressed antipathy to the discomfort of riding downhill, and having previously heard him express his pleasure at the sight of the browsing goats, seized the occasion of a growl to administer an antidote, in all kindness, by crying, "See, what pretty goats!" then causing them to jump at his whistle. The feeling of responsibility exhibited in both instances is akin to the primitive parental.

Bachit Abdullah had ambitions; he also was youthful, sturdy, and good-natured. It was in England that he desired to live. All who come from England have much money and beautiful guns. Their food is rich and their clothing fine.

He remained uninfluenced by my news that it was very cold there, and that he was much better off in Africa. Pointing out that he had sun, and meat, and dhurra, and merissa, and honey, I asked him what more he could want.

His immediate reply was "Garush" (coin)—that all the English had plenty of money. And why did he want money when he had all else? The cat came out of the bag; possessed of one wife, he wanted a number, and it was futile to endeavour to disabuse him of the notion of the universal wealth of the English people or of the desirability of emulating the chiefs of the herds of game we see.

At Khor-um-Asal a fine waterbuck anticipated our advance and cantered away. Many herds of does and immature males had been seen, and the prevalence of the sportsman had left its mark.

But rounding a long oval *maya*, Fadl el Mullah gave the quick signal; I hastily threw myself off the mule, and saw on the far side a herd, including two full-grown buck. Though across the narrowest portion, they were out of range, and a long circuit was taken with the usual anxieties caused by change of position and veering wind. Once they looked up, startled by a scuttling wart-hog, but soon settled down to graze once more.

Worming my way over a small wooded knoll, I lay quite still as the buck came near, fired, and missed unaccountably. I sprang to my feet as the buck bolted off, let loose my second barrel, and brought him down dead as a stone.

Here again my squeamishness was laughed at, when the Arabs ate red, raw tit-bits, steaming hot, from the poor buck's body.

My mule was generally tractable; the exceptions

FLIGHT OF DHURRA BIRDS ON THE DINDER.

WATERBUCK AT KHOR-UM-ASAL.

To face page 108.

so far had been when a pair of partridges lay close in their tussock of grass until the mule's foot came near them. The flurry of the flight and the brush of the wings was startling to both rider and mule, and caused many a narrow escape from a throw.

But there was also a calmness about that mule; she knew her own wants and disliked interference. For the moment she yearned for the simple life. During the dismemberment of the waterbuck, she had learned to love the coarse straw of the *maya*, and there was enough before her for the rest of the year.

The day was hot and the *maya* treeless; my water-bottle hung on the pommel, and I approached to detach it. She divined my intentions differently, and, being content, conceived that my wish was to disturb her enjoyment.

She therefore, without vice or ill-feeling, gently lifted her hind-leg, planted her foot deftly in my waistcoat, and sent me flying over the wilderness of the *maya*. My laughter demonstrating no evil effects, the boys rushed smiling to help me, but their occupation rendered assistance undesirable.

The time of year was unfavourable for studying the flora of the country; in fact, in this locality I only saw one bush in flower, the blooms having the heavy scent of the Christmas-rose, the white male flower and the yellow mate often appearing side by side on the same twig.

The flower of the tebeldi is gorgeous, and in keeping with the majestic appearance of the tree when in leaf, but only the pendent pods are now visible. These vary in size and shape, there being certainly two distinct varieties in this district, one pod being of an elongated egg-shape, about 9 inches in length, while the other is considerably longer and no more in diameter.

Wild-figs, too, were in evidence, but were immature and useless.

It is often a subject for remark that it is almost invariably the European who is the first to spot game. This is certainly not the fault of the eyesight of the native, which appears equal to that of a white man aided by a Zeiss binocular magnifying twelve diameters. On the White Nile, a Dinka pointed out antelope on a distant fringe of bush which it took me all my time to distinguish with the glass.

But unless the shikari is very keen as a sportsman —as was the departed Shereef—if he have obtained his supply of meat, he is liable to go to sleep while travelling, and to lose himself in dreams of an earthly Paradise. Not only his eyesight grows dim, but his hearing, and so particularly was this the case with one of my men, that on three separate occasions he failed to see roan antelope, and also to hear the "cluck" of the tongue which was the recognized signal that game was in view.

There must have been many of these noble creatures in the neighbourhood that day, for, on camping in the early evening, Fadl el Mullah and Bachit, son of Abdullah—both desirous of becoming shikaris, and each with decided opinions and considerable jealousy of the other—rushed to me and informed me that "Abu Ooruf" were crossing the river-bed. Unfortunately, both accompanied me the short distance, and, in spite of my previous injunctions as to silence, at the critical point began to dispute as to whether this spot or a farther one should be the vantage-ground. The high tones of the dispute, and the necessary vehemence of my objurgations, gave me no choice, for on looking over the bank the antelope were on the move 300 yards away.

Bachit was right, for Fadl el Mullah was obsessed with the idea that the eye of a crocodile at a quarter-mile's range was quite enough mark for a moderate gun. The range of my foot as a weapon of offence I hoped would disabuse him.

Opposite, in the blue distance, was the first forerunner—if so one can call such a stationary object as a hill—of the Abyssinian highlands: a solitary granite eminence looking quite out of place, and the sunset shone red on its boulders.

I woke during the night on my couch under the tamarind-tree, and thought to myself what comfort may be in the wilds. So snug was one's bed, so peaceful and quiet the night, that disturbance and danger seemed distant as famine and cold.

My thoughts were broken most rudely; from very close quarters there sounded the impatient and irritable voice of a lion, whose tone was quite different from others we had heard.

The fires were down and almost extinct, for, indeed, such was the effect of familiarity that one had almost come to regard their use as unnecessary. All the men were asleep, and were hard to awaken; but when Abdullah arose I observed a certain celerity in his movements, which with him was unusual, the camel-men following suit. It would appear as though we had intruded on the accustomed drinking-place of his majesty, and I gave way to desperate hopes for the morrow.

There was time to speculate on these hopes, for our wakeful neighbour was in no hurry, and indulged in the airing of his opinions until nature asserted itself and unconsciousness of everything external supervened until the break of day.

The half-light saw us astir; the camels were put under weigh while I started to seek for the complainant of the night. Not 90 yards away we found his spoor, leading us to hope for a speedy discovery.

On approaching the spot in the evening, I had noticed a vulture or two flying low, but in insufficient number to point to anything out of the way.

Descending to a gentle-sloped *khor*, we entered high grass and emerged into a somewhat open space. For an instant something brown moved on the opposite side, and the flash of a hope rose high. It fell, for no lion was there, but just a roan antelope gazed momentarily at us, before covering retreat in the thick growth of grass.

Onward, still onward, parting the herbage,

inspecting each shadow, quiet-stepping and silent we moved, till we stood over the fresh bones of a waterbuck, not a day or two old. Not a moment was lost, but for hundreds of yards the thick bushes were walked through and nothing was seen. Twenty-four hours later two lions appeared to a traveller downstream, and one of them failed to escape.

In certain localities on the Dinder are said to be the somewhat scarce rhinoceros, far more common in East Africa. It was well until recently not to stumble on them in the Sudan, for, while they were forbidden game, they are also of the most truculent character. The presence of mankind, made known to these pachyderms by a tell-tale breeze or casual noise, is sufficient to bring down the charge of the "heavy brigade" with purposeful intensity and exactness. Under such circumstances, even the game regulations of the Sudan must expect to be broken and asperities of officialdom softened. Not being numerous, these animals may be regarded as all but non-existent to the traveller here.

The "white" rhinoceros, whose colour is black, now all but extinct, is never seen here, though in the regions of the Bahr-el-Gebel, on the Congo side, they are still said to exist.

It was in the Zambesi Valley in 1895 that I saw the remains of, I believe, the last individual of its kind that was killed in South Africa, far in the north of Mashonaland. The front horn of this beast was nearly a yard long, and the specimen is set up entire in the South African Museum.

The rhinoceros of the Sudan has a prehensile lip, fitted for gathering twigs, instead of the stumpy, grass-clipping muzzle of its cousin, who, while greatly exceeding the other in bulk, is by no means superior in fierceness and agility.

In the regions where termites infest the country, black hillocks show up amidst the grass. Often these assume the most curious shapes, and it becomes a matter of moment to decide whether they are in reality animals grazing, or merely the structures of the white ant.

I have looked at these objects intently to ascertain their actual character, and been subject to a common illusion. One so often sees that which one wishes to see, and the movement of grass blown by the wind becomes the movement of the hillock in stationary grass, thus giving apparent life to an inanimate object!

In Rhodesia the ant-hills attain an enormous size, being often as much as 30 feet high, crowned by small groves of trees; here they were miniature in comparison.

Clumps of the finger-leaf palm were scattered here and there, and on nearing one Ibrahim made his usual crouching stop, and I instantly followed his lead. We crawled breathlessly under its cover, progressing uphill, and just as we reached it a roan antelope lifted his head from the far side over the palm. My admiration was not reciprocated, and by the time I had walked round the clump he was far away, putting every possible tree-trunk between us, though only half a dozen yards in a direct line through the clump had at first divided him from us.

It is somewhat strange, considering the extraordinary development of the senses of smell, sight, and hearing, and the eternal vigilance of animals who live amongst beasts of prey, that it should be possible to approach so closely, especially with the disadvantage of hard shoe-leather and the laboured breathing caused by movement in strained and unaccustomed attitudes, with the weight of a rifle in one hand.

The Abyssinian frontier was now within a few miles, marking the end of the somewhat hurried journey up the Dinder, and there was a distinct change in the character of the country.

Here three baby lions, carried in boxes on camel-back, were met, accompanied by the slayer of their mother, on his way downstream. The little creatures, with their huge wild eyes, were quite tractable after their few days' captivity, and submitted to caresses with almost the equanimity of kittens. Months later, when grown out of all recognition, one licked my hand through the bars of his cage in Regent's Park, which unhappily witnessed his death and that of his companion some time later.

CHAPTER VI

THE ABYSSINIAN FRONTIER

TEN miles from the frontier lies Abu Ramleh, the post of the department which is devoted to the gradual extinction of the system of slavery in the Sudan. It is by no means universally known that this system still exists in a curtailed form, the Government very wisely abstaining from a sudden revolutionary change which would provoke a cataclysm by upsetting the whole internal economy of the country, and preferring, while giving safeguards for the proper treatment of slaves, and for the attainment of their liberty if desired, to cause the arrangement to die a natural death by cutting off fresh supplies. This it does with remarkable success, aided by the difficulties of travel in the wet season, and in the dry season by the occupation of the isolated spots where water can be obtained. Only one case of slave-running occurred in 1908.

It was in this province that an incident occurred which was related to me in the course of my journey on the Zeraf. Seven slave-dealers were, by what appeared to them a most unhappy accident, caught, with their party of slaves, by a native Sheikh of some importance, on the Abyssinian frontier. Five of them were promptly led up a precipitous rock, and received a slight push ; the rest concerned the hyænas and vultures. The "bag" reached the ears of the Government, but not so the punishment, and the Sheikh was called on to send the offenders for trial. The poor fellow was at his wits' end to comply, but with grim irony exhibited the resource of the savage. In the old days, there being seven men to be accounted for, seven men, of course, would have had to be found, and that they did not happen to be the real delinquents would have mattered as little in Africa as in China. So the Sheikh "bagged" five poor, innocent traders, and sent them up, with the two slavers surviving, to the Government centre. The latter protested their innocence as energetically as the five victims, and the Sheikh so impressed the slaves with the statement that, if they told the truth, horrors unimaginable awaited them in this life and hereafter, that they implicitly obeyed his commands. So it seemed likely that a grave miscarriage of justice would take place ; but there remained a small boy, and that boy, as usual, had an appetite, and that appetite caused a craving for sugar, the temptation of which induced him to talk, and the whole story came out. The slaves were reassured, confirmed the facts, and all came right in the end, the merchants being released, and the slavers saving their skins by being condemned to seven years' hard labour, which was a "mercy" compared with the rough-and-ready justice of their captors.

In the old days of Egyptian occupation the slave trade was enormous and lucrative. Khartoum was the central mart, possessed an immense population, and its wealth and prosperity were extreme. Small wonder that, among a vast proportion of its present population, apart from racial and religious hatred, there exists a resentment, covert but intense, for the interference with a staple and highly profitable trade. Moreover, agriculture is suffering considerably owing to the impossibility of obtaining free labour at remunerative rates, and the "small holder" is being driven off his land. The *sakieh*, too, costs too much, and the native has not reached the level of appreciating an oil-engine and pump, as has happened in Egypt.

In English eyes such servitude is in itself abominable, apart from the horrors which are part and parcel of the system of recruiting. But it is questionable whether the native himself views slavery quite in the same light after the initial experience is passed, which experience, of course, was not invariable. The initial terror of slavery lies first in the taking of slaves, in the horrors of surprise, the destruction of home and disruption of families, the death by murder or starvation of those unfit or unrequired, and in the cruelties and mortality of the march. At the best of times, the negroid in this country is the slave of Nature, which oft turns against him. He has to fight in his home country against famine and tempest, and in many places has hard enough work to pull through.

Of the destruction of individuality and self-responsibility not so much can be said from the practical as from the ethical point of view. As the slave of some Arab he feels no personal responsibility; as a rule he is well treated, and his food is found for him, whether during the period when he puts in his work—no harder than, in any case, he would have done for himself—or during the days when field-work is not needed. This suits his temperament, but fails to stimulate what intellect he has.

I once came across a Dinka Bimbashi of the Sudanese army, whose early days were passed as a slave near Esneh in Egypt. He told me he worked in the fields with the fellahin and was perfectly happy at this time of his youth; he was well fed and comfortable; but, still, said this six-foot-four piece of black energy, "I prefer my life now." With the dignity of rank, the satisfaction of pay, and the chance of a good rough-and-tumble in a small native war, he had reason to do so. He was at Halfa when Gordon was killed at Khartoum.

Another of Zobeir's slaves whom I saw and questioned, a silent, withered old man, said that now he had freedom he could not appreciate it. All sense of self-responsibility had probably been destroyed in him, and he therefore felt lost and bewildered.

When amongst the wilder negroid tribes, it is

difficult to persuade them that one is not a Turk —*i.e.*, Egyptian—the fact that one is white and of the ruling race being sufficient to cause the name Turk to be applied to all.

Such horrible memories cling to the reputation of the old régime, and to the days of the Dervish rule, that the utmost nervousness is displayed by those who come for the first time into contact with white people, as was demonstrated during the latter part of my wanderings, in the Bahr-el-Zeraf.

The Egyptian Government of the Sudan in the days of Baker was in effect a horde of slave-dealers who commanded the sympathy of the ruling classes in Egypt proper, and who were the chiefs of an enormous and infamous organization which utilized tribal warfare and death for the attainment of its abominable ends, and left famine and depopulation in its trail.

The devastating results of the Dervish rule have been already referred to, and it is stated on competent authority that a population now estimated at from a million and a half to two millions amounted to full eight and a half millions before the days of the Mahdi.

The main waterways from Abyssinia are now jealously guarded. The slightest relaxation of this keen watch would be the signal for a revival of the trade, and even now it is possible that a few traders, who are generally well-known and desperate characters, do succeed in getting past. But there is an elaborate detective system—with

A MIDDAY HALT: THE SINGING OF IBRAHIM'S ASS.

To face page 120.

its counterpart on the other side—and the occupation of the water-holes makes a successful evasion difficult.

The slavery police were polite enough to turn out and present arms. It was fortunate that they were accustomed to seeing Englishmen in garb which has seen wear, else such a mark of respect would not have been forthcoming. Weeks of tramping through thorn and scrub, of scrambling and crawling on rough or burnt ground, of the pounding and beating of native washermen, of incessant scrubbing against the post of a camel *maklufa* (saddle), have a sadly deteriorating effect on the respectability of anyone's appearance.

A large *rakuba*, or Government rest-house, was here provided, and was a valuable retreat from the sun-rays during the day. One of the great blessings of the Sudan is the darkness of the native *tukls*. It would seem that it is quite understood that discomfort and danger do not proceed so much from the actual heat of the sun as from either its light or some rays which are not appreciable by the senses. Herein lies the value of advice to wear red or black underclothing to take the place of the pigment with which the skin of the native has been provided, and which undoubtedly enables him to support exposure to the sun in a much greater measure than can a European.

The situation of Abu Ramleh (Father of Sand) is quite charming. The monotony of flat river-bed and long. low, dull coloured bush-line had disappeared, huge stones jutted out of the sand, and rocky undulations were apparent on land. Trees were green and bushy, flowers were more frequent, and at times quite a height was attained above river-level.

Every step forward gave a rise in elevation ; the air was fresher, and there was a certain exhilaration in the knowledge that the dead-level was behind and the joy of the hills ahead, though only to be seen from afar.

Many warnings had been addressed to me to be careful not to cross the frontier, as the consequences might be uncomfortable, and even serious. Strangers are not welcomed in Abyssinia unless their advent be accompanied by official permission, and even that is liable to be questioned by some petty chief.

An Abyssinian prison would not appear to be a healthy place, and abode therein may be indeterminate in length ; in fact, there were rumours of at least one white man who had dared to enter the country, and was still engaged in doing useful field-work for a gentleman of colour and scanty respect for civilization.

A vast area of land between here and Khartoum had long been in dispute between Abyssinia and the various Governments of the Sudan ; in fact, in the fourth century Abyssinian territory is said to have extended as far as the Nile, and the frontier has only been adjusted since the reconquest.

The people in the districts on the other side of

the frontier are not Abyssinian, being more Arab in character and race.

The Khor Abu Ramleh is a considerable feeder to the Dinder on the left bank in the rains, but, like it, now only contained occasional pools. Shining lustrous in the sunlight, many large mother-of-pearl shells lay in the river-sand as we crossed to follow the short stretch of the Dinder which remained for us.

Here is to be found the kudu, with its lovely twisted horns, and I would willingly have remained for a time in the neighbourhood, but the journey to the White Nile was long and hard, and the steamer which was to take me south to more barbarous regions was due in a minimum of time.

Two miles out, travelling silently over broken and stony ground, the spur of an eminence ran slanting down to the river-bank, where it ended precipitously. Rounding its rocky face, we found it the side of a gully, and a patch of loose, dusty soil under the low cliff showed it to be the haunt of antelope, who used it for dusting their coats by rolling. The ground was covered with recent spoor, but, with an appearance of alertness, my Arab in front was dreaming, his thoughts being far away with his wives and his meat and merissa, so he heard not my "clucks," and went straight away on. I gave up the attempt to stop him, and reached for my rifle, but by that time the roan antelope which had stood still, astonished by our sudden appearance not 10 yards away, came to its senses, and, dodging behind a large bush, was away up the hill and lost amidst boulders and trees. It was a well-deserved lesson to me: had I not succumbed to laziness, and had but carried my rifle myself, he could scarcely have escaped. It must be confessed that the temptation is great in the heat of the day, when many miles are being traversed, to shift the burden sometimes to another, but it is often regretted.

The shamefaced shikari, smarting under my tongue, now applied himself to his business, and in my turn I was hardly prepared, when he pointed into the shade of the river-side trees, as we approached from across a bend, for a herd of kudu to break out. They were far out of range, and must have been watching our progress across the bare ground and through the burnt trees for full half a mile.

My own eyes had become pretty sharp through continual watchfulness, knowing I could place little trust in the keenness of the men now the meat had gone back, but I utterly failed to distinguish the forms of the kudu before they made off. To the shikari they were entirely clear, and the superiority of the native over even a trained European eye was again made manifest.

But keen eyesight is by no means the monopoly of the human inhabitant of the Sudan. Time after time I have been surprised at the wonderful vision of the crocodile. Movement, of course, is the great betrayer of the presence of life, and passage along a bank, although almost hidden, will be speedily noted by these seemingly sluggish creatures. Again, I have sat as still as a rock to the leeward of buck without being discovered. So, as the crocodile here were numerous and large, I determined to stalk them. To show oneself, or merely one's head, at the edge of the bank was the inevitable signal for a rushing dispersal into the pool-waters below. So I chose the cover of a thick tree, overhanging the water at a height of 30 feet, at a spot where, over a distance of 300 yards on the sandy shore 80 yards opposite, were a dozen or more reptiles, two lying directly in front of me.

Hidden by the foliage, I crawled inch by inch, worming along prone under the cover of the thick tree-trunk, so that at no time could more than a portion of my helmeted head have shown over the edge of the bank amongst the leaves. They were also to windward, so no question of their powers of scent came in. Yet nine-tenths of them, firstly the most distant, and all apparently sleeping, detected the movement, slight and slow as it was, had divined it to be due to no other creature than man, and had crawled into cover.

Only the two which were hidden entirely by the tree-trunk remained, and a bullet went plumb into the neck of the nearer; his enormous jaws opened wide, his tail moved convulsively, taking him just into the water, where he lay still in the shallows.

This day was a day of disasters. All sportsmen must have such in their memories, when the ill-chance of circumstance seems to prevail. But every such circumstance carries its lesson, and it is the ready remembrance of such which gives the value to experience.

Midday had arrived; we were still on the tramp, with the heat at its height. Strolling along in the river-bed, lazy and unconcerned, were four kudu. These creatures are by no means common, and seem to frequent only favoured localities. Their size is considerable, and the large spiral horns aid in making them one of the handsomest antelopes known. In the Sudan the horns do not appear to attain the proportions that they do in Rhodesia, and none of those seen in this district seemed equal to quite ordinary specimens which I secured there.

I got in my shot quite well, and the best kudu fell plumb, and remained stretched out on the sand down the river. The others stood staring to look for the cause, but, knowing their scarcity, I forbore to fire, one example sufficing. Carelessly rising, I instructed the boys to descend to him, and turned away while they ran by the bank for an easy way down. A shout made me turn; I saw the buck move, rise well to its feet, get into its stride, and follow its friends with despatch! The dead had arisen. A flying shot, almost hopeless at the distance, failed to turn it; it scaled the bank just ahead of the men, and entered the forest.

The probability is that the bullet had just grazed its spine, and for the few moments knocked it senseless; and in this connection it is possible that I had made too little allowance for the effect of the midday heat on the cordite of the cartridge. It is a well-known fact that heat causes a gun to throw high, and it is said that 6 inches error at a 100 yards is not too much to allow when the sun is at its highest.

I urged my men at a breakneck pace on its tracks, but they were lost before long on the stony ground. Feeling it possible that, with the tenacity of life exhibited so often, even when mortally wounded, it might have made a final struggle and succumbed, I followed the direction in which the spoor led, and not half a mile away, so true our direction had been, the troop of four animals burst from cover and finally disappeared. So ended my opportunity of matching a Rhodesian with a Sudanese mate.

We were now right on the frontier, and blue in the distance rose steep, isolated mountains, appearing, in the usual African fashion, accidental and out of their element. And yet they seemed almost systematized in arrangement, and constituted a chain of natural fortresses stretching away down the frontier-line. One of the nearest of these was named Gebel Magnun (Mount Fool), and on my return journey I found it a most fitting synonym for those who accompanied me.

The two boys were with me, and their rank disobedience was the cause of the last of my troubles. Bachit, keen as mustard, spotted Abu Ooruf (roan) coming out of the opposite bush. Swiftly we ran downstream, far back from the bank, to the spot they were quietly making for. I crawled through the grass, and rested still as a mouse, with my sights fixed on an excellent buck now well within range; my finger was pressing the trigger, and a thousandth part of a second remained, when, with a startling change of movement destructive of aim, they whisked round with a flash and galloped away.

Turning round now, the cause was apparent. The two boys, whom I had sternly commanded to wait behind under cover, had longed to be in at the kill, and appeared on the bank, utterly wrecking my chances. My feelings baffle description; I took Bachit by the arm and showed him the *kurbash* (hippo-hide whip). Knowing his fault and deserts, he readily responded, "Haddir, Effendi" ("All right," "ready," or "certainly," "sir"), and prepared for a thrashing without the sign of a murmur and as a matter of course. Gebel Magnun as a name always sobered him after.

The backs of these boys and of many of the men of different tribes are seamed and scarred by the *kurbash* in a terrible way; when asked what the marks are, they are intensely amused, and their cause seems considered an experience of fun and enjoyment, a recollection inspiring happiness and laughter. They are said to be due to ebullitions of playfulness after a *diluka*, or dance-feast.

CHAPTER VII

FROM DINDER, AND NILE TO NILE

After hunting from sunrise to sunset, with only an hour of rest, it was by a great effort of will that I brought myself to face the five hours' journey by moonlight on the way to Roseires.

The journey had to be strictly planned, for the distance was about seventy miles; water was already exceedingly scarce, and the places where any whatever could be obtained were but three in number.

So, tired as I was, those five weary hours in the darkness had to be patiently plodded through; even the moon had nearly deserted us, and only the catlike eyes of the Arab in front could see any sign of the faintest of tracks. My route lay almost due west across the Blue Nile, through Roseires to Renk on the "White," a distance of nearly 200 miles through a nearly waterless country.

I had brought four goatskins (*girbas*) from Singa for use on these cross-country journeys, and uninviting they are to English ideas. Black, sweating, and gorged, they smelt of the tan, and a new one would part with a scum which gave taste to the water. For this reason old ones are best. Great care must be taken of the skins not in use, as they are liable to be punctured by a small insect. When once this occurs, or they are torn, it is almost impossible to mend them. Many Government folk used iron receptacles specially adapted for carrying on camel-back, but to my mind they are by no means so practical, save in the amount that they carry. The water was half boiled by the sun on the iron, and rough treatment caused many a leak, whereas the *girba* by its sweating kept cool, adapted itself to inequalities of surface, was lighter, and took up no space when empty. The rude thorn had certainly to be guarded against, and my thirsty mule was at one point convicted of tearing a hole in a *girba*, vainly endeavouring to gather the vanishing drops.

In general the camel-men would place their *girbas* in a safe spot just behind the *maklufa*, the only disadvantage being that through the pores of the skin some exchange was likely to be effected between its contents and the sweat of the camel.

At midnight we camped for but four hours' rest. How those four hours raced! Still dark when we rose, the coffee awakened one, the going was pleasant in the fresh morning hours, and the track not too bad.

A small *gebel* appeared before us, skirted by trees, and roan antelope raced round the patches of grass.

Piercing the tree belt, a broad space opened out at the foot of the hill, which is called Maganou; here was a large sloping "pan" in the shelving rock, containing what by the Arabs was popularly called "water." In no place was the depth more than 2 inches, and it was rapidly drying. From events that I saw, it must have been quite ammoniacal; the black mud which the drinkers disturbed supported squashy vegetation which covered the main part of the surface. Yet the camels and men rushed down to it, no after ill-effects being experienced.

The *gebel* was most picturesque; its rough, precipitous sides were covered with rank vegetation; in every nook and corner amongst the boulders bushes and baobabs sprang. In the foreground the camels and natives gave the requisite factor of life.

For twenty weary miles of slow travel through all too thin trees and great open plains that seemed never to end, we plodded along.

A track had been made by the Roseires authorities, but of all the travesties encountered in life this was the worst. True, it gave us the way, but, rather than ease the going for camels and mules, this was rendered far worse, and the animals obstinately refused to employ it, preferring the inequalities of the softer soil to the hard-trodden and burning hot track.

The kind night fell on the last stages of our trek; mile after mile appeared longer; even the blithe

Fadl el Mullah looked sour, and Bachit lagged behind. The camelcade straggled to a mile-long line; the water-skins grew empty and flabby, and camels complained.

Then in the gloom the dark form of a mountain appeared, and for miles we skirted it, passing at last to its farther end, and reaching, thank God, the "slavery post" of Gebel Gerri.

Even here there was so little water that it was carefully kept for the use of the police, whose posts are neatly arranged and tidily kept, being fenced in with grass and well swept, and for the folk of the small village near.

Now only six hours away is Roseires, where I am to cross the Blue Nile, nearly 400 miles from its junction with the White Nile at Khartoum, on a still harder journey. The river was struck some miles above the town, and the vegetation was an extraordinary change to that among which I had been for some weeks. It was bigger and thicker and denser. Instead of thin, naked trunks of wide-apart trees were masses of thick foliage reaching the ground. The tebeldi-trees were numerous, and formed a particular feature of the locality. The ground, too, was hilly, and the track had expanded into a broad, smooth road along which the beasts travelled gaily, scenting the river and looking for rest.

So here was once more civilization; days and weeks of only Arab companionship were past. One had visions of enormous baths, easy-chairs,

ACROSS THE BLUE NILE FROM ROSEIRES.

HALT AT GEBEL MAGANOU.

To face page 132.

and last, but not least, a complete change of diet. I had travelled in a day and three-quarters what is usually given three days, and so looked forward to a rest in Roseires with friends I had found there.

The position of Roseires is pretty indeed; the town is high up on the steep hills of the bank, and looks over the swift-flowing current rushing between many great rounded boulders. The mere movement of water after still, sandy river-bed and quiescent pools was refreshing. So an invitation to fish was accepted. It involved the rowing of a Noah's Ark up the stream for a fourth of a mile. The Ark was built up of four-inch thick planks, the oars were the paddles of Brobdingnag, and the stream was the giddy Blue Nile. We were carried far down ere we won our transverse way and crawled up in the slack of the current. Then a wild dash across to an islet, and the Ark was deserted on the strand.

I had read of the experience Baker had with these "cow" fish, which run up to 70 pounds weight and give grand sport. So I watched my two friends as they handled their heavy bamboos and live bait. Hooks were heavy and long in the shank, and soon a fish of 12 pounds weight came in.

One fisher had gone to the opposite side, and I was aroused by a despairing shout, "Come here, Tangye, and help; sure I have hooked the devil!" But to call me the line had been slackened, and his majesty cunningly took up the hint, and when I arrived was away. More than once afterwards gear was taken clean off or hooks straightened out, showing the size of the monsters. They are excellent eating.

On the opposite bank lay the gunboat, protecting this main road from the frontier, which had taken a sudden dip southward from Abu Ramleh, and was now many miles up the stream.

Under an adjacent tebeldi-tree worked a native blacksmith, his goatskin bellows blown by a patient small boy. With their crude tools these men can do very good work, and some are remarkably clever.

Not far away some young waterbuck were being tamed for transmission over the 400 miles to Khartoum and to Cairo. They are herded with calves of about the same age, and are gently induced to submit to a tether, by degrees being brought to follow the calves and be handled.

News came that only four days remained for me to cross over to Renk, 116 miles to the west. Being considered a fair five days' journey, it was obvious that one night's rest was all that could be spared among the charming surroundings of the Assuan of the Blue Nile, as it was laughingly styled. But little of a health-resort can it claim to be, and one of those hosts who so kindly received me lay dead not long after of blackwater fever.

Nor could I accept a suggestion which was made, that I should shoot a rogue elephant which was causing much damage to crops a day down the river. So the evening saw the camels ferried across; all my dark friends of the chase were left behind to give themselves up to the pleasures of town, and the blackness of African bush in the night-time swallowed up a greatly diminished company.

Trophies had been despatched to Khartoum—or left for despatch, for they arrived there months later—by camel to Singa, and thence by native boat to Khartoum. It is needless to say that the low state of the river and continual sand-banks entered into alliance with the one cry inevitable in Africa. From the "Mangwana" of Mashonaland to the "Bukra" of this country, "To-morrow, to-morrow," it is always the same over the whole length of the continent, and one marvels at anything being accomplished at all.

Yet above all, in this country, arrangement and planning are necessary. No one can start on a journey haphazardly without running considerable risk. In the 116 miles lying before us, only in two places could water be found, and two stretches of forty-six or forty-seven miles each had to be traversed without replenishment of water-skins or refreshing the camels.

So every available *girba* was filled in the fresh running stream of the Bahr-el-Azrak. The camels themselves took their fill, and the long trek was fairly begun. The full moon after a while made travelling easy by night, and the camel-men chanted their weird songs in turn to keep touch with each other the whole length of the line. Close behind me the first stanza began, tuneless and indeterminate as the Arab song is, and the last one came on from invisible distance, articulate, tiny, and far.

But it was weirder still when their singing ceased, and one could only hear, and that hardly, the soft pad of one's own camel sliding silently under one, all other footsteps being inaudible even in the stillness of the night.

Yet the tense silence was not quite unbroken; in the most desolate places there seems to be life. Here and there the crickets chirped, and the night-birds sometimes called, while the cry of the foul hyæna, wandering like a hopeless evil spirit, broke upon our ears and reminded us of other travellers by night who are neither seen nor heard till their chosen moment comes.

Here is the home of great loneliness; the country is foreign and strange, and the hour is eerie. Human dread of dead silence and darkness is born of the imminence of the unknown. This is all round one, and in the undefined bushes at one's feet, or those shadowy forms which seem to move in the course of one's progress, there lies a weird spirit of threat and of mystery.

Approaching a tree, in the branches of which a few spots where the blackness is thicker are dimly discerned, the very fury of sound seems let loose; to all points of the compass it spreads, yet diminishes quickly, leaving the world to its silence again. It was merely the guinea-fowl roosting, and escaping the too near approach of mankind.

Of necessity the morning start was early, for at

least thirty-two miles had to be covered to bring us halfway between the two sources of water-supply by next evening. Gebel Agadi provided the first. It is strange that these lonely heaps of granite, erupted pimples on the face of an otherwise dead-level earth, should so often mark water. Sometimes, indeed, the spring issues in places on the height of the *gebel* itself, to the convenience of leopards and baboons which haunt the rocks.

But Gebel Agadi, or the collection of heaps known by that name, is also tenanted by man—to me a new form. Perched on and amongst the great boulders of the hill were scores of their grass-covered *tukls*, or huts, much resembling those seen in Rhodesia, but minus the centre support which exists in the latter, and which robs them of some of their spaciousness.

It was raw man, savage, barbarian, causing my camel-men to appear, as they felt, high in the scale of civilization. My Berberi servants seemed on nearly a plane with Europeans, and all scornfully called the villagers "Arabs." The negro in America insults his brother by calling him a "nigger" or "black man"; here the same principle entered, for all were supposed, more or less incorrectly, to be Arabs of different degree, though strictly, in this case, a probable aboriginal ancestry renders the villagers' right to the classification doubtful.

The tribe is the Ingassana, and possesses distinct characteristics, being more substantial in build and darker in colour. The men are faddists in hairdressing, many styles being exhibited. Some wear it arranged in a multitude of neat, narrow plaits running concentrically round their heads, or from the crown downwards; others, a protruding "friz" on either side of their forehead.

They did not submit to the Government until 1903, and are remarkable for the extraordinary shape of the swords or knives which many of the men carried, and which are also used by the Berta tribe, one of which is illustrated. These appear to be as useful and as much used for the cutting of grass as for warlike purposes; a weapon unusual

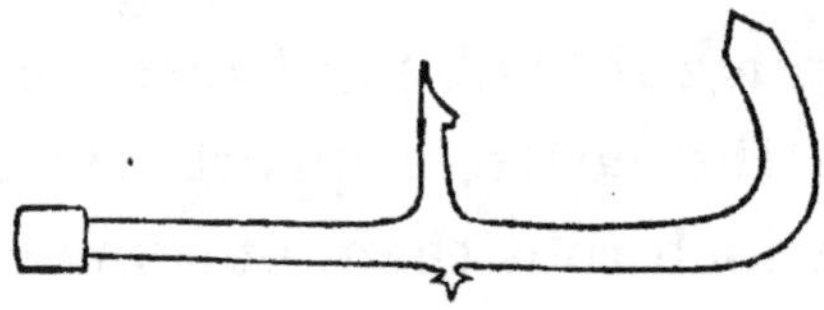

in Africa is a species of boomerang, which, however, differs from the Australian, inasmuch as it does not return to the thrower. Boomerangs are mentioned in the history of Queen Hatshepset, of the Eighteenth Dynasty, who obtained them, with gum and other natural products of the Sudan, by an expedition from the Red Sea coast to the Land of Punt.

Several huts were in course of erection by the Ingassana in the police quarters, grass being brought in for the thatching, which exhibited the usual aboriginal expertness. It was noticeable that the roofs were constructed on the ground, and then lifted into position, in place of the framework of the entire hut, roof and all, being constructed first.

Forty-six miles of country lay between us and the next water, a burning and thirsty stretch. A blackamoor added himself to the party, leading the way with his donkey. It was but recently that this short cut had been opened, the old course trending to Soda (delightful name!), far to the south, then upwards again to Gule, so the native's assistance was welcome.

The men, knowing my strangeness to this country, appeared surprised at my naming the direction in which to proceed, and various places and *gebels* which came into view. They knew not the use of compass and chart, and the burning-glass equally astonished them when applied to a cigarette.

The blackamoor, too, was a cheerful soul, despite a solitary eye, and tender inquiries as to the cause of the raw, unhealed wounds on his back were once again the signal for contortions of amusement. He had probably been too gay after absorbing a skinful of merissa, and met with a well-deserved punishment.

In the driest of country I was surprised to see guinea-fowl, many and many a mile from water. The natives seem to think that, like the desert jerboa, they need none; but the remembrance of the nightly procession of thousands of birds on the Dinder discounts such a statement. It is more likely that they know of some spot where some water remains which has not caught the eye of man; yet it would seem a rare chance that over hundreds of years, in districts where water is more precious than gold, even one such spot should escape.

On the route farther north, from Hillet Abbas over to Singa, in various places were to be seen artificial reservoirs of considerable size, formed to retain the rain-water for a time, but they were long since dried up when I saw them.

From nearly a hundred miles north, right down south to the banks of the Sobat, the country was closed to the visiting sportsman, who becomes a mere bird of passage; for one-half of this area was reserved for the sporting purposes of members of the army of occupation and officials, and that to the south was the much-needed game reserve. So not even *gedad* were in danger from me, and my breakfast was short of its most pleasing feature.

The whole tract of country has an infamous reputation for lions, who appear to be bolder than elsewhere; yet I had difficulty in prevailing upon the camel-men to make a good fire, and each night I awoke to find it extinct. The men sleep by their camels, and perhaps hope that camel would be preferred to man—a belief I should hardly think justified.

Two treks of twenty-three miles each, with but five hours' rest from 11 p.m. until four in the morning between, and with slow baggage camels, was a tiring experience. My fine Abyssinian mule had long ago given out, and was incapable of carrying a load; so my seat had been taken on the camel carrying my kit-boxes, and weary indeed was the way.

Miles ahead, amongst the low line of bush, was a small blue excrescence, which one saw for a moment and lost again. On we went, as it seemed, for hours, the hill looking bigger and bigger, yet never appearing to come nearer. Every African traveller knows the exasperating effect of approach to a hill of considerable size, and the false impression the atmosphere gives as to its distance.

For the moment the hill left our minds. The blackamoor suddenly stopped, and I followed suit, as he looked forward, as I thought, somewhat anxiously, and into the bush on the right. Yes, there was movement, but what? "Zeraf," said the Arab behind me, but he was in error. It was a party of Arabs on camels, slowly wending their way through the bush, as though wishful to escape our notice. "Bad people," said the blackamoor, probably because they did not belong to his village, and came from the hills to the south, or because they were visiting nomad Arabs. So we proceeded; but right on their tracks, where they probably crossed over the path, came a quite different sight, but which equally claimed our attention.

Quietly strolling across in the line of the Arabs was the first lion I had actually seen. He seemed to be following the trail of the strangers, and only appeared for an instant, about 300 yards away.

But, alas! the stern rule of the country forbade. "Officers' Reserve" had been genially forewarned in Khartoum, and nothing short of self-defence would have been held to justify an infraction. So the great footprints were looked at with interest, and the minds of all were quickly recalled to the heat and the thirst and fatigue, and the mocking great *gebel* before us.

Miles farther on there appeared patches of grass all cut short, and to my ears came the plaintive cry of a goat; thank goodness, at last we were nearing the goal. Small children ran shyly away with their herds, or dodged behind bushes and grass. We overtook men on the march, and the *gebel* came suddenly nearer. So used had I become to the view of the hill being merely a vertical plane, that to see its face develop prominences and hollows seemed strange; and when the hill was actually near it seemed to come rapidly toward one, making up for its coyness at first.

That Gebel Gule should be seen from afar is not to be wondered at. It is 1,050 feet high, and close upon three miles long. In the days of the kingdom of Sennaar, Gule was the chief town of the province, but now has fallen from its high estate, and the headquarters of the district is Keili, nearer the Abyssinian frontier, across the present line of which extended a portion of the old Fung kingdom, a descendant of whose Kings gave his name to the village of Sheikh Idris Wad Regab.

The inhabitants number about a thousand, and are either Hameg pure or with a dash of the ancient Fung in their veins.

I had brought the monthly wages to the police at both Agadi and Gule, and this proved a very

HUT-MAKING AT GEBEL AGADI.

APPROACHING GEBEL GULE.

To face page 142

good introduction. The corporal in charge went to some trouble to obtain milk and eggs for me, and the official hut in the middle of the compound provided shelter. But the hut was of brick, and gathered and held all the heat it could find. The door certainly faced away from the sun; the window was the merest apology. Then, the sun of the great continent is as clever as a buffalo: if it cannot get at one direct, it comes round a corner. The pith helmet is a sufficient bulwark against the heat from above, but the sun gets over that by rebounding his rays from the ground, and thus coming from under; or he mixes them up with long grass, to bombard from sides, back, and front.

Here in this hut, being unable to penetrate the front-door by direct route, he aimed his shafts at the naked, precipitous cliff of the great granite hill, which radiated them unceasingly during the day on to the camp, robbing it, too, of all benefit from the less hot northern wind.

Still, rest for a spell we were forced to, especially as the camels struggled in full two hours later, and threw themselves down on the hot ground exhausted. The men disposed themselves as though they had a week to spare, and many were the grumblings and objections when I insisted that a further ten miles must be accomplished before midnight.

For the sake of the animals, a start was deferred until eight o'clock—well after sunset—and we passed to the north of a vertical rock of great height, apparently set up on end, called the Marid. The moon was not due; the track was quite new, and could not have been followed without a guide from the considerable village at Gule. These men seem to see in the dark almost as well as a cat; at times the new blackamoor halted and peered round about, but I was too tired to question. The camels were walking dead slow, and my back was half broken, so that when midnight and rest came I could scarcely await the make-up of the bed. From the previous morning we had come sixty-five miles, and the camels were feeling the pressure.

During the following morning a zariba was passed, the thorn-branches being particularly strongly arranged in proximity to an unfinished well. This was evidently a Government under taking, and marked the halfway between Gule and Renk. But it was deserted, and on my arrival at Renk I learned that a fortnight before a lion had actually jumped the zariba, dared the fire, and had seized the poor well-sinker and carried him off, wounded and torn by the thorn. Inexplicably, the lion then dropped him, and the man was taken into hospital, where he recovered.

All of this country is covered with the densest species of thorn the world knows how to produce. The kittir bush-thorn in itself is the worst of its kind. To penetrate even a short distance into it is to run the greatest risk of being "bushed," for it is impossible to see a yard or two in front.

This, then, is a favourite hunting-ground of lions,

and the whole neighbourhood of Renk is renowned for them. By chance I neither saw nor heard one, and as a matter of fact I was glad that my much-needed sleep was undisturbed, though I woke up to find that the tired camel-men had let the fires down.

The track had been cut as a Government road through the kittir bush. One could almost believe that the old Romans had recently arrived, so straight it proceeded over hill and down dale, visible miles in the distance ahead—a rut in a carpet of bush. Here the plain was abandoned, and the ground was undulating; the vegetation doubtless felt the influence of water, if only in the atmosphere.

The evening found me within so reasonable a distance of Renk that I could easily have run in; but it was preferable to sleep away from the river, in freedom from the mosquitoes of the humming river-side. The sight of a bootprint in the dust impressed me almost as vividly as Friday's did Robinson Crusoe.

It may appear strange to those at home that one can *smell* water, but no signpost was needed to tell me the end of my trek was at hand. Five miles away one breathed great gulps of the water-freshened atmosphere; I revelled in it—almost bathed in it. Yet to the traveller fresh from Europe it would have been parching. A gaiety spread over the whole camelcade; the animals quickened their pace and seemed glad.

So freshened was I that I found walking the

easiest mode of progression, greatly to Abid's delight, for he expressed aversion to my arrival in camp on a baggage camel, saying that only "Greeky merchants" did that, and that it was out of the question on the score of dignity.

The kittir bush ceased, and open plains followed; then came the dried-up plantations of dhurra, a few *tukls*, then more, until quite a populous centre appeared. Farther on was a long line of regular poles which brought Europe within speaking distance, and the wires led me on to the *mamuria*, the post-office, and then the White Nile I had left weeks ago.

A swarm of donkeys appeared on the bank, followed by a welcome sight—a British soldier, a corporal of the Royal Engineers, just off on some weeks' journey south to inspect a few hundred miles of telegraph-wire.

The ten miles' walk in the morning had been refreshing, though Abid expressed his opinion that Englishmen were unwise to walk so much, as is their habit, particularly when they could just as well ride—a truly Oriental reason. The corporal required two looks at the travel-stained tramp, in clothes worn into holes by camel-riding and crawling, disfigured with soil and black ash, boots with the surface scratched off them, and a three days' beard; so it was a matter of relief to feel that one was not taken for a peripatetic Greek merchant, and to hear the words: "You seem to have had a hard journey across."

CHAPTER VIII

MAN IN THE SUDAN

At this point it may be well to glance at the history of some of the tribes who now inhabit the countries we enter, or what is known of or guessed at in regard to it.

The student inevitably comes to the conclusion that guesswork greatly preponderates.

The earliest remains found, probably neolithic, long anterior to earliest Egyptian history, are in Egypt and Somaliland, and a mummy now in the British Museum, found in Egypt, on the west bank of the Nile, though light in colour and fair-haired, lies on its side, with legs bent up against its body, and head supported, in the identical position of some prehistoric remains uncovered at Harlyn Bay, Cornwall.

The main points of theories naturally rest, firstly, on an assumption that the human race originated beyond the Euphrates, from thence spreading over the world, perhaps in the first instance in Africa in the form of pigmies and bushmen, then Hottentots, who have in the course of known history been driven farther and farther back into forest or desert retreats. The negro now appears as an existing type, of more advanced physical features, but still low in the human scale, and approximating the ape in the comparative length of arms, early ossification of the cranial sutures, and the prognathic jaw.

There are evidences of mixed negro and pigmy blood in the Jur and Bongo tribes, the negro predominating; and the pigmy is more evidenced in the Mombottu.

The influx of a light-coloured Caucasian race pushed the negro onward also; but, being a stage or two higher than the pigmy, he was less inimical to the new-comers' influence, and in some cases allowed them to cause more or less modification on coming into contiguity, rather than undergo exile or extermination, the resultant representing the negroids.

Dr. Weule of Leipzig stoutly contests the theory that the negroes have joined in the accepted movement from Asia, preferring to think them indigenous to Africa. Some support may be lent this by the fact that the most characteristic negro types are found in regions remotest from Asia; but to this argument may be opposed the obvious fact that, being farthest away, they have been less exposed to the effects of later ages of Asiatic influence.

It is interesting to note *en passant* that a connection has been suggested between the names of the sons of Ham with various districts of these contiguous areas. *Cush* is assigned to Cush,

Ethiopia; *Mizraim* to Musr, the native name of Cairo (see Gen. l. 11, where the place of "the mourning of the Egyptians" for Jacob is therefore called "Abel-Mizraim"); *Phut* to Punt; and *Canaan* to the land of the same name. Various divergencies from this stock, of different degrees and rates of progress, may account for the types of humanity existing there to-day, apart from the Semitic element.

The main elements influencing the races as we now see them include the pigmy, the negro, the Arab, and the descendants of prehistoric aboriginals, represented by the opponents of the ancient Egyptians, such as the Nubas of Kordofan, the Barabras of the Dongola-Assuan tract, and probably others.

Both negro and Arab in the pure state are non-existent, and both have become differently modified from the accepted standard type.

Of the origin and identity of the Nubas and kindred peoples little can actually be hazarded. Generally admitted to be of Hamitic origin, they appear to have an original ancestry neither Arab nor negroid. It has been suggested, on account of certain characteristics of the old Himyaritic (*himyar*, dusky) language, and the customs and institutions of Yemen anterior to Islam, that this is of African affinity. The reputed settlement of a Himyaritic race south of Assuan and elsewhere might seem to support this, and Herodotus definitely refers to the co-operation of straight-haired *Asiatic* Ethiopians with the curly-headed ones of Africa, who differed only in this respect and in that of language, thus involving people from both sides of the Red Sea. That this deduction is not unopen to doubt is evidenced by Mr. Stuart Poole's mention of the description in the Septuagint of the "land of Gesem (Goshen) in Arabia" as applying to an Egyptian province on the Arabian side of Egypt; so that the term "Asiatic Ethiopians" might in like manner apply to the inhabitants of that part of Africa adjacent to Asia. Herodotus speaks also of their habit of covering themselves with red earth—a practice of Kordofan Nubas of to-day, in common with some of the negroids. The long bows of these folk were of palm-wood, and their arrows were tipped with stone "of the sort on which they engrave seals," probably the desert agate, still in such everyday use for the making of beads.

The difference in colour, which dates from earliest history, between the descendants of these ancient inhabitants of the Nile, the Nubas and Barabras, is great; and the same difference exists between the more primitive species, the brown-yellow bushman and Hottentot and the black northern pigmy.

Sir H. H. Johnston holds that the Nubas are negroid; but Gleichen is positive of the contrary, in spite of their blackness of skin.

To possess a black skin does not necessarily mean negro descent, though it might be collateral with it; but its occurrence is arbitrary in regard to its obvious intention—protection from the sun's heat and light rays. Perhaps the most plausible suggestion is that damp heat produces a darker colour than dry.

The Nubas and Barabras retain their own languages, which are allied, and also speak Arabic; they appear by no means too sound as Mahommedans, and I concluded, by observation and talk with my servants, that respect for Mahomet was only skin-deep.

Fungs and Hamegs are classed as negroids by Sir H. H. Johnston, and exhibit certain primitive customs, such as the use of the boomerang by Ingassana, phallic worship within the last century, and other uninvestigated ceremonies, among the Fungs; while a Caucasian type is said to have been observed among the Berta. These tribes offer a field for study which may throw light on the degree of a far-away relation with Asia.

The well-known tendency of Sudanese tribes to migration or travel is a difficult factor in coming to any conclusions, but it may be well to bear in mind that the country inhabited by these latter peoples is on the confines of the Land of Punt, whence some authorities say the early Egyptians first hailed, before going north, and is near a trade route to the Red Sea more ancient than history.

One learned authority places the Land of Punt across the Red Sea, while others consider that both sides were embraced, including Yemen and Somaliland; and it is legitimately to be argued that all these races were originally akin to the Semites at a period anterior to their appearance in Africa.

The practice of smearing the body with red earth, referred to by Herodotus, and also decoration with chalk, is not confined to the Nubas, being general among the Bantus. The Nandi exactly follow the example of the Ethiopians of Herodotus, painting one side of the body white, the other red. I remember a Bari, far up the Mountain Nile, evenly tinted all over a rich dusky red, not an atom of black being visible. The Shilluks follow a scheme of facial adornment with chalk which has some counterpart in Australia, but there used to indicate mourning.

Pliny refers to the red earth plaster in regard to the Ipsodoræ and others, living on the west bank many days south of Meroe, and speaks of a nation, more distant still, who were 8 cubits in height—say 7 feet 7 inches—which is not unknown amongst modern Nuers. Strabo speaks of the Heleii, or "marsh-men," in a similar location, and these historians might almost be writing of to-day.

To Diodorus, speaking of the riverain blacks in the heart of Africa, is reserved one of the most exact accounts, although he omits reference to great height. He says they were flat-faced blacks, with curled hair; fierce, cruel, wicked, and bestial. Their bodies were foul, and their nails long, like claws. Their weapons were clubs, spears, and hide shields; their food, flesh, milk and cheese, marsh-fruit and sesamus. Many of their women went naked; their

FAR UP THE MOUNTAIN NILE.

dead were buried in their houses. All these constitute features which describe the Nilotic negroids of to-day.

Speaking of the extraordinary journey of the Nasamonians, Herodotus makes it clear that these ancient Libyan adventurers reached the Bahr-el-Ghazal and its morasses, at that time inhabited by pigmies who have now retreated to the Congo forests. Nero's centurions were the next recorded visitors, many hundreds of years later, and apparently reached the neighbourhood of the Great Lakes.

It is fairly to be inferred that the negroid races which inhabited Ethiopia then, remain to this day, and are generally in identically the same state of uncivilization that they existed in at the first dawning of history. The first mention of them in our earliest records speaks of the land as the "Ta-Nehesu," which has precisely the same signification as the name "Sudan," the "country of the blacks."

The enormous lapse of time which is involved as necessary to the development of such distinct types from a common ancestry is thus made a little appreciable.

Diodorus cuts the knot by stating that the Ethiopians were the first people who ever lived, so the idea of a black Eve, which makes one to shudder, must be debited to this worthy Greek!

But among the negroids there is also much classification. Those of the Sudan are greatly behind the tribes who have wandered southward, and who have won their way onward as far as South Africa, founding kingdoms and impressing their individuality wherever they went.

It would seem once again a demonstration of the survival of the fittest, for the more virile and intelligent divisions would be uncontent to remain in localities scarce fit for beasts, much less for man, and would leave them to those who trusted to inaccessibility for safety. The marshes of Southern Ethiopia provided this *in excelsis*, protected these negroids from intermixture with the Arab immigrants, whose blood has so profoundly permeated many of the races of the north and east, and developed physical characteristics which mark them from all other men.

Among the most prominent tribes of the marsh class are the Dinkas, Shilluks, Nuers, Buruns, Anuaks, Bari, Shuli, and Jur, and as representatives of races who by their surroundings have been kept in the most primitive condition—not necessarily the most unintelligent or unresponsive to effort—they are very interesting.

The natives of Australia are low in the human scale, and, apart from the almost bestial powers which they share with the bushman, they are merely undevelopable. No one who has come into touch with a Dinka or Nuer who has had the benefit of contact with a higher civilization, could say so of him. Farag Effendi Abu Zet, now resident near Singa, is an example; a born soldier, he is covered with decorations, was promoted on the field to his rank of Bimbashi for his extraordinary bravery, and, retired on account of wounds, now finds peace as profitable as war. They are not undevelopable, but simply man in the raw state, perhaps nearly as God created him in the first instance, and just unadvanced. The Nuers are likely to remain in this condition until circumstances develop which one cannot with certainty foresee; only drainage will render it possible to break down the barriers which the character of their country imposes against fuller communication with the outside world, and though the first step in this direction is being taken, it is difficult to estimate what is involved.

Distinct divergence is existing between the various divisions of Nilotic negroids. The Dinka has impressed himself the most, and extends his area, while the Burun and Anuak have remained stationary, and the Bari retrograded from the once prominent condition which was exerted so powerfully against Baker.

The most noticeable feature amongst these peoples is the effect of environment and occupation during ages which are almost geological in extent. The enormous height of Dinkas, Shilluks, and Nuers, is caused mainly by length of leg, a provision of obvious utility in a country which cannot be traversed without wading, and where the art of transfixing fish with a spear whose shaft is bent by a cord is practised waist-deep in the crocodile-haunted river.

CHAPTER IX

TO THE LAND OF THE NEGROID

EVEN in the Sudan, with its financially limited resources, conditions ameliorate and progress is made, and in two years Renk had much changed for the better. A low, desolate, fever-stricken patch of crude land, treeless and bare, with a swampy, stagnant *khor* blocked with vegetation and breeding myriad mosquitoes, had been so altered that it was scarcely recognized. A landing-stage with a broad approach dignified the bank, a grove of trees graced the road—such is the power of African soil, sun, and water; and the official residence, though of that abomination in hot countries, corrugated iron, was sumptuous in comparison with its predecessor. In place of the swampy *khor* was a clear surface of water, but in one respect it retained its sinister character.

Here the native women come down to replenish their water-pots; tucking their wraps tightly round them, they wade knee-deep into the stream, fill their vessels, and struggle back to the bank. But not always; unperceived, a narrow, long head over there has quietly risen and taken the bearings of the unhappy woman: with directness achieved by long practice, exact aim is taken, and the villainous body shoots invisibly under the water. A scream, and the woman is gone, to be held under water, perhaps stowed in a hole, and devoured at leisure.

On the roof of a disused building is the roughly stuffed hide of one monster who had haunted the *khor* to the villagers' terror, and who before he was shot had in a short space of time killed and eaten three women.

The native population has greatly increased in this neighbourhood, and representatives of various tribes have made more or less permanent residence here. Large fields of dhurra greet the eyes on coming near Renk, and the number of *tukls* was testimony to the results of sympathetic government in this *mudiria.*

In the *khor* might be seen Arab fishing-boats, whose owners found ready sale for their captures. The abundance of fish in the White Nile is always a matter of wonder. Particularly up in the "sudd" districts the river surface is dotted with rings where the fishes are rising, in countless and unceasing numbers.

One variety, the aigel, in particular, is perfectly eatable by Europeans, and is almost tasty, attaining remarkable size. The fish-market being the river-bank, the Arabs are enabled to keep their wares fresh by refraining from killing, and by tethering them by a rope through the lip to the boat. "All alive, O!" on the Nile is a cry with foundation in fact.

We here come into touch with the great negroid races. The Dinkas are particularly in evidence, this being approximately the northern boundary of their country. They belong to a group of tribes possessing many characteristics in common, apparently evolved through the peculiarities of the country which is to them home. Just as Nature steps in to provide the mud-fish of the Dinder with lungs on retreat of the water, so she approximates man to the style of the stork in the regions of the marsh. The Nilotic negroids, such as the Dinkas, Shilluks, Nuers, Baris, and Buruns, though showing minor variations, exhibit a common type, which is more traceable in relation to Dinkas and Nuers than others. The Dinkas appear to possess the more diplomatic character, though their ability in warfare is less, and their habitat has extended enormously over great areas. Their country ranges from the north of Renk up the east bank to near the country facing Fashoda, where some Shilluks join in. On the west bank the main body of the Shilluk nation extends to the great bend of the Nile, where the Sobat and Bahr-el-Ghazal combine with the main stream.

Then south, on the west bank of the Mountain Nile this time, the Dinkas once more appear, now being faced by the Nuers, who spread to the east far beyond the Bahr-el-Zeraf, and are hemmed in by the Twi Dinkas on the south. But in the Khor Filus, opening into the Sobat, is a section of Dinkas of whom more anon.

Intense blackness of skin is a much-pronounced feature. In the Dinka it is perfectly wonderful; no grease-paint compares with its marvellous tone! The impression given is that they are immensely tall, but this is partially aided by their slimness of build and the comparative length and slightness of their limbs.

An average taken by the late Dr. Pirrie gives a height of 5 feet 11 inches, and a maximum measurement of about 6 feet 3 inches. I took no measurement here, but that of the chief of a band appeared to be much in excess of this figure.

Marsh and river dwellers, who subsist much on fish, they partake of the same dispensation which has given the stork his long legs, and common to both is the habit of resting on one leg.

No more remarkable sight exists than that of a number of naked young men, with the sole of one foot placed at the side of the neighbouring knee while they balance themselves with the aid of a down-pointed spear, the tip of which is protected by a piece of soft ambatch-wood. This attitude is reported by Dr. Seligmann to have its counterpart among the Toro tribe of New Guinea.

A notable was due to call at Renk on his way up-river, and a native dance was arranged for his edification. He was unable to stay, and, rather than give disappointment, his place was taken by me.

It was a motley assembly, consisting of Arabs, some runaway slaves—respectable old gentlemen with the tarbush (or fez), and white cotton shirt worn outside the white drawers—then a band of Shilluks, and another of half-naked Dinkas, the chief of whom was dressed in resplendent attire, and, to the best of my judgment, came near 7 feet in height.

The Shilluks from the opposite side of the river possessed the same habits, and their hair-dressing was as remarkable as their appearance in general. With a view to warding off the attacks of mosquitoes, they cover themselves from head to foot with wood or cowdung ash, fortified, I believe, with cow's urine, taking care to attend to their faces. The effect is most ghastly, for only their lips and a space round the eyes are free from the ash, which gives an appearance of decay to the skin.

This practice extends amongst many of these tribes, and was in particular use with the Nuers. In both cases, wood not being always available, dried cowdung is used in its place, the heaps of burnt ash coming in handy as mattresses for the night's rest.

Their dance was a study in savage hostility, a contrast indeed to present-day warfare. They transported me back to the Iron Age, which indeed is their stage of development. Forward they came at full speed, bending low with their spears in queer, spider-like rushes, here and there crouching to ground, retreating, and coming on fiercely again. Their delight was extreme, and so was the dust they created.

The Arab dance differed entirely. Rather than

THE ASH-COVERED NEGROID AT RENK.

THE "CROC" THAT GOT INTO TROUBLE.

To face page 160.

warlike in character, it was quite unsensational. Four men and four women advanced toward me, retired backwards and came forward once more, keeping time with short steps and a hopping shuffle, and a bend of both body and knees. Eventually the men approached closely, then the women supplanted them, two kneeling before me, two standing, all chanting and casting weird glances until a shilling was placed on their foreheads. In the meantime the respectable old gentlemen with the tarbushes and serious faces became comic in their intenseness and vigour.

I learn that the laws of the Dinka are of a most intricate nature, drawn up in a well-defined code, and dependent on sequence of reasoning. Many provisions have resemblance to laws detailed in the earliest books of the Bible, and comparison with the Babylonian records of Hammurabi—the Amraphel of Genesis—might bear interesting fruit.

When it is realized that the method of government, to every possible extent consistent with British ideas of humanity, is to apply native law, the tax on the powers of a conscientious Inspector can well be imagined, and the difficulty in this unhealthy country is to avoid frequent changes, with consequent loss of efficiency.

One speculates, when primitive man is before one, as to whether the early man of Genesis exhibited such characteristics as these—whether Adam, Cain, and Abel, rolled themselves in objectionable matters and wood-ash to keep off mosquitoes, and dressed their hair in clay, cowries, and cowdung.

One is accustomed from babyhood upward to consider Adam and Eve as somewhat refined personalities, with white skins and good looks, albeit, through sheer force of circumstances, objectionably careless of clothing. But what foundation have we for such charming ideals? As creations, in mind they were certainly crude; as mere products of Darwinian evolution, they would be but a single advance beyond brutes. The Dinka is distinctly ahead of his parents in Eden, for while they yielded to instinct, just as savages might, they had none but the simplest codes to follow—simple through mere paucity of population; but the Dinka has many more temptations, has propounded elaborate laws, and on the whole fairly abides by them, such as they are! He is no more naked than were Adam and Eve in the Garden, and, where the Tree of Knowledge grows by the civilized river-side, follows their later example. So we see our first parents as poor, untutored barbarians, quite unable to appreciate their manifold advantages, and as a disheartening failure!

The name Adam is still so widespread among the Arab tribes that it may seem a surprise that the name of his wife is not heard as we know it in Europe. But Adam, of course, was barbarian, and he and his sons would consider mere woman unworthy a thought, much less worth naming in history. So the deficiency must have been rectified by some grateful descendant, but where he got the name Eve from we may puzzle to know. It sounds so nice and so very poetic, and one thinks how sweet and affectionate and savoury and clean she would be; but her prototypes among the Dinkas, and their manners and customs, do not bear this out, and my thoughts turn to the black thing in front of me, sitting in dust, lean, ugly, regardless of parasites, and making butter too dreadful to think of.

My Arabs had stared at me in amazement when they were asked for the "camera," not understanding the word, and I had to fall back on the Arabic equivalent for "black box," inasmuch as I found they had mistaken my request, and deemed I required them to bring me the *moon* (*kamar*), and thought me unreasonable! But at Mellut, where the *Nasr* called for a short time, the Arab colony exhibited an ancient acquaintance with the camera, no doubt through the agency of enterprising tourists who seek refreshment of mind in the journey through swamps and the land of ferocious seroot flies.

A few score of miles up the river the men would have stood on the bank shaking their hands up and down, and bending their knees in synchrony, to keep off the "evil eye" of the boat from their dhurra and herds. But here it is Eve who evinces the same superstition; the thought of the eye of the serpent assailing her, she scurries affrighted to the gloom of her hut when she sees the black magical box pointed at her.

The small girls bring one nearer to home. They are just as inquisitive, just as shy and half frightened at anything strange, as the wee lassies of England. After gentle persuasion they peep through the camera "finder," spy their sisters, shriek with half-scared delight as they rush headlong away from the incomprehensible thing—only just for a short distance—and then come back again.

The steamers are fired by wood cut from the bush which fringes the river, and the increasing demand is causing the gradual denudation of the banks by the small colonies of Arabs that are maintained at the many "wood-stations" formed for this purpose. An impertinent stranger might hazard the opinion that one of the first duties of the Woods and Forests Department might well be the replanting of the large areas which have been despoiled of their timber, only too often in the wasteful native fashion, which cuts the trunks high up, leaving the stump unused to decay and rot. Coal in briquette form is brought up and used to a small extent, but even with the opening of the Port Sudan railway to the Red Sea the cost is practically prohibitive.

The main enemy of fine timber in this country is fire; the tortured twists of the straggly trunks bear witness to the fierceness of the flames which lick up the grass around them. Small chance is there for seedlings, and doomed is the tree whose bark gets once burned through. Here are tree-stumps smouldering, days after the swift rush of the con-

AN ARAB DILUKA.

NATIVE CANOES CARRYING DHURRA.

To face page 164.

flagration; there on that black, burnt ground is the delicate tracery in white ash, undisturbed by the breeze, of every twig of the skeleton of a tree, fallen victim.

Little puffs of smoke fitfully shoot up, and the predatory birds swing by. Sometimes the vermilion flames will run a race fifty miles up the bank with the persistent north wind. Days after the sweet green shoots appear, and the buck come round to feed.

Methods of combating the ravages of this scourge are the study of the Woods and Forests Department, and blocks of country are reserved wherein no man may shoot, while patches in strategical positions are cleared. In the Sennaar province this seems to have met with a great degree of success, 9,552 acres having suffered in 1908, as against 65,000 in the previous year, though perhaps the Department would not claim credit for the whole of the difference.

After the effects of fire, the destructive pranks of elephants have most to be reckoned with, for the greater part of the wooded banks of the river in elephant country had suffered from their attentions. Here, there, and everywhere were hundreds of the slender trees broken and bent to the ground, where the leaf-eating monsters could more easily feed. At intervals were trees uprooted whole, a fragment of broken tusk occasionally lying by as evidence of a penalty paid.

Being sarcastic by nature, the elephant refuses

to recognize any suggestion that he should be able to discriminate between trees and iron telegraph-poles, which suffer accordingly; and in the rains he has a peculiar aptitude for utilizing the line of the wire as a footpath, leaving tracks 2 feet deep, which, when masked by vegetation, are discovered later on by the unfortunate white man, to the detriment of his shins and the hindrance of his progress.

Though, generally speaking, the timber is poor, it grows to considerable dimensions in some localities. The hard "sunt," when large enough, makes a decent substitute for mahogany.

Apart from the use its bark is put to for making rope, the tebeldi has an important function in Kordofan, and may constitute a valuable asset to its owner. Being generally hollow, it acts as a natural storage reservoir for rain-water, which is used for drinking purposes, and keeps perfectly good for a considerable time.

Rubber is being experimented with in various latitudes, and there is reason to hope for considerable development in its cultivation.

The samr and marakh, whose shoots are beloved of camels, are used by the natives in the making of fire by friction; while the kittir, abominated of mankind owing to its thorny denseness, partly redeems itself by also providing bark as material for rope.

The great deleb palm, scooped out, forms the canoe of the Nuer; the pith-light ambatch, the buoyant raft so easily carried on his back. Many of these are seen on the way up the river. Natives hurriedly scurry across on their ambatch as they see the steamer approaching, half immersed in the water, and daring the hippos and crocodiles.

Not far in the distance excitement was shown by a party of Dinkas on shore, who watched a canoe whose movements were erratic and jerky, apparently governed by some outside influence. Approach rendered visible three cylinders of wood at considerable intervals, but possessed of common inspiration in movement. At one moment they dashed like surface torpedoes for a quarter of a mile up the river, with the native canoe hard after them.

Changing their course, they rushed down and across, and then up again, churning the waters. Many a time the paddlers darted their frail structure aside, till at last the black head of a hippo appeared, gradually exhausting his great life away.

The hunters did not welcome the idea of a white man accompanying them in their boat on this exciting quest; every thought was required to dodge the infuriated beast, who, attached by harpoon to the rope, was dragging the dead bulk of the long line of floats with such wonderful power and speed under water. But they welcomed the *bundukiya*, or rifle, which would transform the work of another twenty-four hours into a matter of minutes, and great were the shouts of approval.

The courage these men show is extreme. Far away down the stream at the tail of a mid-river inlet, where the water is slack and the depth is but slight, they see the rounded forms of a dozen dark giants. These lie half covered with water on the soft sand of the river-bed, basking and sleepy in the heat of the day, never dreaming of peril. Strange that these great pachyderms, links with the bizarre monsters of the past, who need fear no other four-footed creature, should be prey to the puny human in one of his lowest forms.

Silently, slowly, three men in a boat float down on the herd, one in the bow poising the harpoon, one amidships, and another at the stern, with paddles held tight and muscles tense with the imperative call to act suddenly, strongly, and swiftly. A pink baby beast lies half submerged on his mother's broad back, and a big bull is beyond.

The current-borne object floats by the big bull: a sudden bend of the body, shooting forward the arms, and the black statue becomes instinct with muscular life. But the waters are raging. At the instant of thrust, back darts the canoe, and its occupants row for dear life, for the outraged quarry has no hesitation when, recovered from shock, he discovers his enemy. Not always is a retreat effected, and the huge jaws crash through the canoe, when woe to the man who is trapped. Many hours may elapse before the tail of the rope is brought on to the bank, and, wearied to weakness, struggling vainly, the hippo is drawn within reach of the spears, which soon put an end to his trials. Up here they have to be dealt with as vermin, the damage they do is so great in the native plantations of dhurra.

After all, civilization and invention have achieved something; the bullet is quicker in action than the primitive spear.

It is almost incredible that as late as **1831** a geographer should calmly describe the hippopotamus as being well known to have cloven hoofs, the tail and mane of a horse, and in size to be equal to a large ox. Yet this is the description which the Rev. Dr. Russell endorses, having taken his inspiration from Herodotus rather than from fact!

The seroot flies had not been so numerous for some reason. No one who has not undergone their attentions can properly appreciate their effect on the nervous system. A penetrating buzz, intensely intent, springs into a rushing existence of a million miles an hour. Sight does not easily follow it; the sound ceases for a fraction of a second, unlocated; then a red-hot needle is plunged into parts of one's anatomy which were thought amply guarded. Clothes appear to be as protective against *X rays* as against the powers of this vicious busybody. So the next time the warning note is heard, a dash for the "meat-safe" is made, from the inside of which disappointed insects can be seen glueing their heads against the mesh of the wires. They have one redeeming feature, inasmuch as it has not yet been demonstrated that, as do the tsetse, they harbour microbes inimical to man.

But to be regarded as meat by anything is objectionable, and inspires a certain resentment. I remember positively hating a vulture when I wakened one day, to find it soaring over me with mistaken impressions. And only an innate courtesy once prevented my expression of a sense of bad taste, when a most hospitable old cannibal Nyam-nyam lady, after cutting the throat of a fowl at her hut door as I entered, remarked on the satisfactory appearance of my figure as compared with that of my spare-built companion. It was flattering, but carnivorous; moreover, I felt that no advantage lay in transmutation.

From Renk, which is 300 miles south of Khartoum, we plodded patiently up the White Nile toward the country of swamp and of negroid. Many lazy hours passed by until a slight rise in the bank appeared on the eastern side in the distance, with a grass-covered islet or two. The forest had retreated far back from the river, and was scarcely to be seen. Merely flats of dried swamp just occasionally rose above level, but stretched beyond vision. The prospect was not fair, and its loneliness forced itself on one. Far down the west bank a tiny protuberance rose as the steamer forced onward at its sure, sluggish pace. The beat of its paddles astern, carried over the water in regular cadence, warned the crocodiles at the edge of the stream, and sent small clouds of brown teal whistling onward. The "Father of Teeth" strolled about pensively, head cast down, deep in thought, and with long, grave, deliberate steps; his hands were

A WOOD STATION.

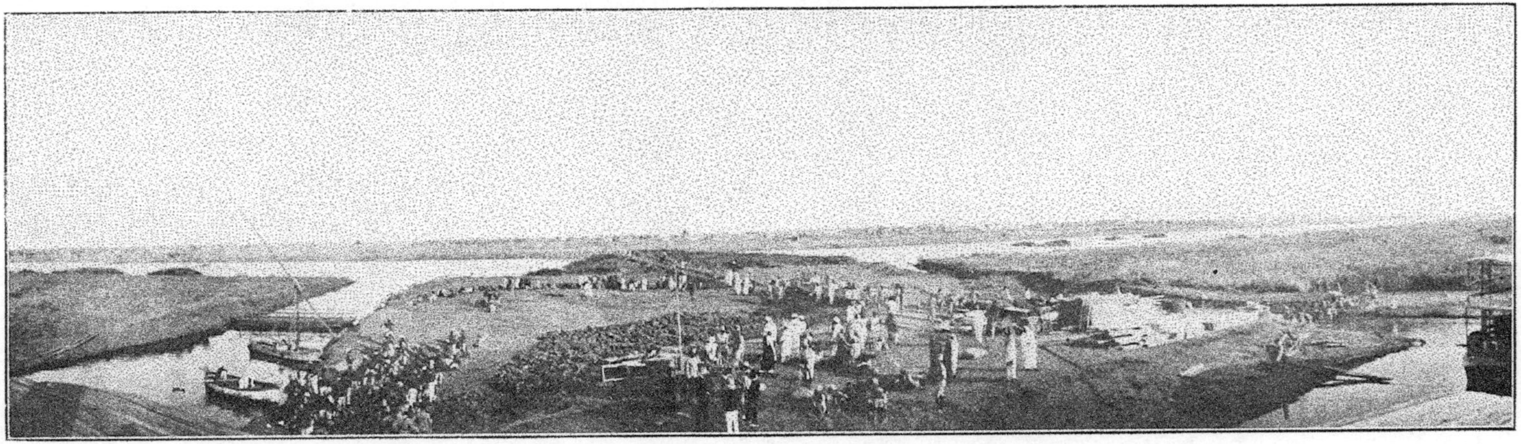

FASHODA (KODOK).

seemingly under the tails of his coat, yet he was only a marabout stork seeking food.

Cattle appeared at intervals, grazing; black dots grew out on the wastes, showing man; the protuberance took shape in the shimmering sunlight, and became a brick house with a cane fence around. Irregular buildings around it, a few heat-stricken trees on the bank, with some vegetation beneath, the Governor's house stood high in a land where a molehill would count as an eminence. Still well in mid-stream—for the river is wide at this point—we made for a spot where some nuggars were gathered on the outer side of the western of the two islands. Dropping the sandals, or barges, on which were some Sudanese soldiers bound for the south, we made fast.

Even Fashoda develops. The long line of the settlement crowning the bank some hundreds of yards away had been joined to the island by a causeway, where once a steel boat dug its way over the shallowing *khor*. A tramline brought truck-loads of freight, pushed by a varied assortment of blacks. Long lines of swathed women marched down to the stream with their earthenware pots, for the water is bad in the stagnant *khor*. Women they were of all sizes, and ranging in tint from jet to the colour of coffee. Wee lassies brought gourds or small pots, and gravely mimicked the work of their mothers, wrapping their scanty garments tight round their thighs as they stepped knee-deep in the stream. Their little backs straightened as they strolled proudly away, holding the pots on their heads, gaining erectness of carriage, and commencing the hard share of work which falls to African women. In Mashonaland, spilling of the load is reduced to a minimum by the floating of leaves on the surface; here there were no leaves to float. On the opposite shore, at the foot of the grass of the eastern island, the crocodiles watched.

A circle of women sat by with their wares, forming a miniature market, welcome to soldiers and sailors; while an infantile Adam, naked as when he was born, stood on the bank, as our boys do at home, with a stick and some twine and—who knows?—a bent pin, earnestly fishing. Surely this was a king amongst black men who strode slowly along and lazily looked at the boat with an air of detachment from all his surroundings! Long, spare-limbed, and lanky, a cloth knotted over one shoulder, he carried a spear. His hair was felted into a flat, fan-like creation at the back of his head, while in front it was short-cropped and reddened. A neat row of cowrie-shells bordered the forehead, while the whole was surmounted by three ostrich feathers, the middle one white. A broad band of white followed the line of the jaw from the ear, the top of which was adorned by a circular disc of sardine-tin, and a large ivory bangle was worn on the arm. All round about him was labour, but no notice took he. The world might be wrecked, but so long as his district remained, what mattered it him? A picture was brought to my mind of a start from

Tewfikieh, when my steamer was fighting against a north wind. She was blown hither and thither, not succeeding in facing the gale; for the draught of these vessels is small, and the freeboard and top-hamper great. Time after time she cannoned the shore, burying her nose in the rush-covered bank. The sturdy *bahari* tumbled ashore with their rope at the stern, and struggled in vain. 'Boreas *v.* Bahari' was the name of this great tug-of-war, which was evenly matched. Lackadaisy, close by, were half a dozen blacks looking on as one might at a sheep trying to nibble a tussock of grass beyond reach. Lend a hand? Not a bit of it! The sailors might pull themselves stiff before the noble savages would interfere, and a British carpenter would as soon think of assisting a plumber! Beyond building a hut and tending their cattle or fishing, work does not lie in their scheme of existence, and so long as they remain as they are, an absolutely primitive people, with small imagination and less in the way of ideals, there is no impulse to tell them why it should. Their conditions, too, before British protection came on the scene, as elsewhere in barbarian Africa, have been hostile to work, save the tending of cattle and fishing. Stern logic of facts has caused them to hold themselves ready for war, to protect their property and lands or to raid in their turn, to absent themselves from their villages while their women-folk, always at home, did the work.

It was thus easy for them, so long as pressure of

circumstances was absent, to fall in with the plan of non-interference with the more regular labour; and, now that their energies are not required for warlike purposes, it is necessary to divert them into directions which will ultimately lead to the creation of necessities hitherto undreamt of, and consequently the obligation to work, and thus take a useful part in the world.

This is the basis of education here, and the spectacle of a hundred or so Shilluks engaged in levelling disused embankments was evidence of a beginning, in whatever light they themselves may have regarded it.

It is extraordinary what progress has been made in winning these people's confidence and in gaining more control; it must have been difficult to make them believe that conditions had changed, and that they were no longer subject to slave raids and extortion. Their numbers, as seen on the banks up the river, have increased enormously; from not far above Fashoda to the great bend of the river the villages seem unceasing, while their herds have increased twentyfold. For many years the policy of dealing with these tribes has been in the hands of one Governor, whose consistent and enlightened ideals have been fruitful of good.

A long line of buildings half a mile in extent it made, this Fashoda, or Kodok, as they now choose to name it. To the north was the Governor's "palace," on the site of the camp of Marchand, his garden in some sort remaining, but all else dis-

A SHILLUK BEAU.

SHILLUKS LEVELLING OLD EARTHWORKS.

To face page 174.

appeared. Behind were the earthworks he raised, and some rugged brick buildings used as stores, and built in the days of Egyptian possession.

Straggling southward were the *mudiria* and court-house, flying the emblems of Britain and Egypt, and guarded by diligent sentries who challenge all comers; *zaptieh*, or prison, with the soldiers' "lines" in regular array; then a large open space of cracked soil, which at times smelt as though hundreds of years of dark population had fouled it; lastly, the less precise but still orderly lines of the *suk*, or market, and the native quarters, which were expanding visibly.

Fashoda presents its worst side to the new-comer. One would judge that it backed on the river rather than fronted it. So little arrangement appears to have been made in regard to town planning, apart from broad lines, that irregularity seems to be fashion, and it forms a contrast to the orderly neatness of Belgian formations up-river. Still, great odds were encountered, and existing dispositions seem to have been made as much of as possible. After all, it is merely a mound with the river in front and marshland behind, wet indeed in the summer.

Malaria is rife, as may well be expected, but improvement in this respect is apparent even here, as the result of regulations following on the invaluable investigations in regard to the breeding-places of the mosquitoes.

At the back of the town is a well-ordered hospital

in charge of a competent doctor, with a motley collection of patients from far districts and near. Shilluks, Arabs, and Nuers were amongst those who profited by the facilities given, and each and all wondered why they did not get well on the first dose of medicine. This constitutes one of the great difficulties in treating the native. Treatment seems to be held as a species of magic, the effects of which should be immediately visible, so regular attendance of out-patients is hard to obtain.

Surgery is attended by similar difficulties; patients cannot believe that it is well to lose half a leg in order to save the rest of the body. In South African hospitals a species of fatalism is common. If a man once give up hope, which a white man would cling to, he says he is going to die, and forthwith puts his intention into practice, and *dies.* It is similar here, and no steps will prevent them when once they have made up their minds!

Their own medical practice is a mixture of elemental knowledge, quackery, and superstition, many sensible methods being led to more by accidental results than by reason or principle.

One feels struck by the position in which a servant sometimes places his employer in this country in regard to his personal relationship. He appears, especially if his employer be long resident in the country, to expect him to take a generally paternal interest in him and his condition of life, even after he has left his service. It may be an unrecognized relic of old days of slavery, when power even over life and death seemed to involve some amount of a compensating obligation, and the absence of responsibility for actions or thoughts on the part of the servant required an assumption of this by the master.

If he be wronged—particularly, of course, by a fellow-domestic—he comes naturally to his employer to be assisted, and in some instances is apparently willing to allow his life to be more or less regulated by his master. I have been told, in the case of the latter being much trusted, that having more or less by innuendo given it to be understood that he had a desire to get married, a servant may patiently wait for his master to "find" the wife (who has generally, nevertheless, been delicately indicated), and on receiving the information that one has been chosen or found, and that he could marry her, may reply with an impassive face, looking directly before him without changing a muscle: "Haddir, Effendi" (Ready, sir); "I will not disobey your commands"—ostensibly taking the information as an ordinary order or instruction, all in the day's work, and to be carried out without question. All the time he would be bursting with delight at, perhaps, getting the very girl he had coveted.

There is no question of courtship, and, probably, at first little affection in the matter; it is a matter of physical appreciation in most instances, with judgment as to utility thrown in. For woman is an asset in Africa beyond other places; not merely a wife, she is largely the provider.

> "Man works from sun till sun,
> But woman's work is never done."

Up at the dawn, she draws water, often carrying her burden long distances; prepares food and makes beer; grinds the corn, which she has largely sowed and ingathered; tends the babies she slings on her back; and often accompanies her husband on long expeditions, carrying the impedimenta of travel while her lord is unburdened except for his arms.

Yet it would be sweeping to say that, at least after marriage, there is not affection; this could not be said of brute beast, let alone human beings, and though doubtless the level does not in general reach the height that it does with more civilized peoples, the finer sentiment must exist, if but crude, and great joy is often shown on the reunion of long-separated members of a family.

In regard to their children, this is much more developed, more especially in regard to the boys, for girls do not rank with them. Parental instinct overmatches uxorial. But if matrimony be a serious undertaking in England, not less so is it in Africa; it may be infinitely more so on account of plurality, a responsibility hardly appreciated by us, unaccustomed as we are to utilize our wives as beasts of burden, and only, sometimes, to consider them as monetary investments! As this responsibility may even in Africa become somewhat onerous, it is

BELGIAN POST AT LADO.

modified among most races, but not among all, by a power of divorce almost American in its facility, but mainly in favour of the man.

So matrimony is not to be lightly entered into by the inhabitants of the Sudan, even in respect of one wife only; there is considerable formality to be observed in the nuptial proceedings; an expensive feast for numbers of relations is considered necessary; a dowry has to be provided for the bride, who has, moreover, to be supplied with new clothing, and, indeed, also the mother-in-law! It is quite easy for an Arab to spend a sovereign on each garment, and savings are long in increasing.

On the other side of the causeway we may come across prisoners in chains, under guard, doing the light work of the sanitary department, drawing water for the use of public buildings and staff, and by no means too discontented. Some Abyssinians stand up as we pass, having come down the Sobat, perhaps in the hope of evading military service, a fact which causes them to be returned whence they came, to avoid complications. Many of these men are martyrs to "itch," and are thus most unwelcome visitors.

At the back of the Governor's house is the north-west angle of the old Egyptian earthworks, now only just observable, and bounded by old buildings of brick. These are relics of 1871, when the Egyptians, after much previous difficulty, finally conquered the Shilluks. This was the site which Marchand occupied so bravely and anxiously during nine months, after his brilliant journey across Africa to what still was the land of the Dervish, then at his last hour of resistance.

In the centre was a large tree, which had fallen and looked hardly tidy. The reason that it was not cleared away was a spiritual one. In Maori parlance it was *tapu*, and dared not be touched without giving offence to the Shilluks, who regarded it as representing the heart and centre of their nation.

Indeed, the sacred character of this spot was one reason for the continued occupation of Fashoda. The tree has been since cleared away, and a sapling was planted elsewhere. But the sapling died, and, strangely enough, a shoot from the root of the old tree sprang up, so that the emblem of national existence bursts into new life. It is to be hoped that a savage appreciation of this event may not also involve administrative difficulties.

On the far side of the earthworks a solitary cross appeared, marking a grave, and looking lost and forlorn in the sweltering landscape; and down by the side of the *khor* were the quarters of Egyptian employés, who, unfortunately, stand the climate but poorly. It is a strange fact that the Egyptian, accustomed to heat, albeit dry, undergoes the severity of Sudanese climate much less easily than does the European, and displays much less fortitude. One poor fellow had lost his wife many months before, and was in great trouble because her relatives in Cairo required that her body should be transplanted to her native soil. His correspondence on the subject had been protracted, and the expense he was being involved in enormous.

Nevertheless, he dared not face the return to his family without having complied with their wishes, and the corpse was exhumed after months of interment, and despatched the 1,800 miles northwards to Cairo. The sacrifice he thus undertook would probably entail a protracted sojourn in exile, far from the "fleshpots" which his soul yearned for. The phenomenon has been observed here of a corpse resisting the apparent effects of decomposition, much in the same way that has been noticed in Irish bogs. When the body of Lupton Bey was exhumed on the occupation of Omdurman, it was mummified and perfectly recognizable after the lapse of years.

Across our path marched a tall, erect figure, black as sin. Long muscular thighs protruded from the ox-hide garment hung over her shoulder, as a mother of Shilluks made her way home to the hut far away to the west.

That mysterious West—what lands and scenes are lit up by the sun as it throbs its way daily across the great continent! From the long-limbed Shilluks it goes onwards to Nubas in South Kordofan, hilly and wild, but half brought under restraint and control, where the villages perch on the hills, and every man's hand turns against that of his neighbour; then over the regions of French Sudan, Lake Tchad, Nigeria, and on to the sea. It sees countless myriads of human beings, whose lives are often dependent on the caprice of a chief, whose existence is always up against the edge of the sword, but who gradually, slowly, are being rescued by civilization from aggravated uncertainties as to life and to liberty.

The career of the domestic cat is full of moments of worry, lest a dog come along to endanger her life; wild "beasties" suffer the same apprehension. Only civilized man lives in any degree of calm peace of mind—that is, moment by moment; his barbarian brother shows the same aptness of animals to live composedly during the periods of quiet, without giving undue thought to the morrow. When existence is so chock-full of uncertainties, it is well to be able to dismiss them from mind and live in the present; otherwise abode on earth would be divided merely into two phases of unhappiness—the misery of apprehension and the torture of actuality.

To stroll into the *suk*, as the civilian native quarters are called, properly meaning market, gave food for amusement. Here were Arabs and Greeks with their frail shops full of wares, mainly for native consumption. A Greek trader, unkempt and untidy, came slouching along, ready to purchase a tusk, to contract for constructive works, or to head a trade expedition in the interior.

Living much as the natives do, adapting themselves to circumstances as they find them, the Greeks contrive to live and make small money where an ordinary European would starve. They

NILE FISH AT FASHODA.

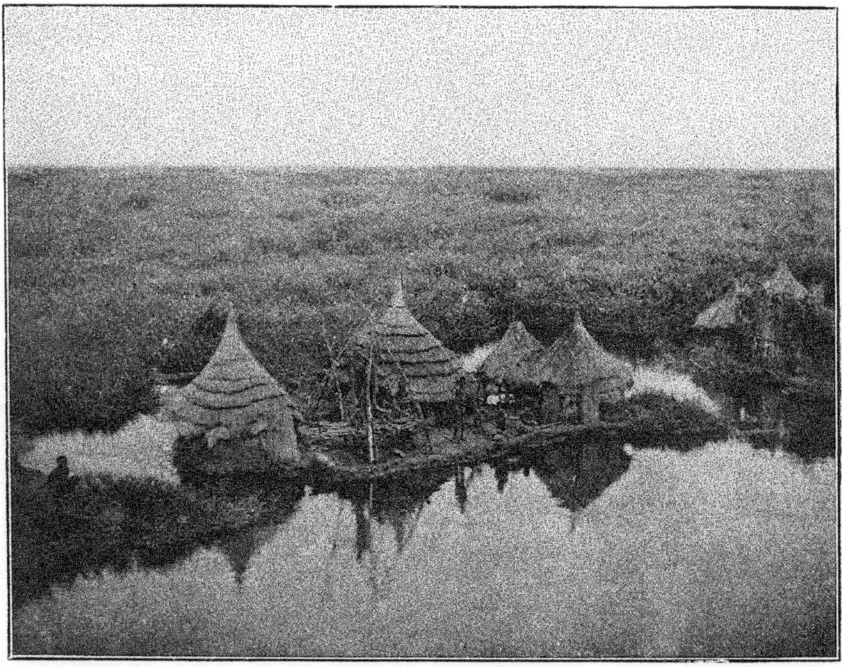

NUER FISHING VILLAGE.

To face page 182.

find their way everywhere; pushing to a degree, if not too reliable, their assistance is invaluable. But their very powers of self-adaptation render them little respected by natives, who scarcely consider them white men, and look with contempt at the "Greeky."

Housewives surrounded the stall of the butcher's shop, crowded with quaint pieces of meat; drapers made much of their cottons and cloths. The long sheet which provides the dark lady with a dress of unvarying fashion in shape was greatly in evidence, while the shop hard by had its little panniers of lentils and other produce of the soil.

Native salt, dirty and hard, in cones, with admixture of the dirt it was evaporated on to, was on sale as a valuable article of barter, as were brass wire and beads.

On the shore a strange sight was provided. Far down-river a number of Arabs arrived with their boats. They were fishermen by trade, making their living by catching and selling the great *semmuck* of the Nile, and were engaged in skinning and scaling them as the purchasers came round. The size of these fish is enormous, and their flesh really good. I have reason to believe that it palls on the taste after many months' diet; but to me, fresh from the tinned food of the march, it was luxury. Many were 7 feet long, and their wide-open mouths were immense.

Now came a small flock of sheep, brought in by travelling Arabs, who expected a price which they never would get in Fashoda. Having marched many miles, their regret was extreme.

Walking homewards, a most characteristic spectacle presented itself. A long line of perhaps twenty men, of all colours and sizes, stood facing roughly north-east; together they knelt and prostrated themselves, mumbling their prayers and performing the whole ceremony so religiously observed by the Muslims. I have often been struck by the accuracy with which they face Mecca; they stand the test of compass and map most remarkably. Can one imagine a party of navvies in Britain knocking off work five times a day for the purpose of performing devotional exercises?

Here in Fashoda there did not appear to be the nightly disturbance by hyænas to anything like the extent I observed on the Blue Nile. For at Singa, newer in foundation and surrounded by bush, these animals haunted the place in the night. Incredibly bold, the mad barking by dogs of the village would herald the robber, who would now and then steal a goat which had been carelessly folded. Apparently fearless of man, though not daring to touch him, they would steal past our beds like grim shadows—on one occasion even jolting the bed of a sleeper. Familiarity breeds contempt, and no qualms were experienced after the lapse of a few nights.

Yet there appears to be one species of a far different character. Three soldiers came into Renk and declared they had been attacked by a monster hyæna, black in colour. They escaped with difficulty, and exhibited the butts of their rifles, which had been smashed by the powerful jaws of their assailant. I was told that this large black hyæna may be found in Kordofan, and that he is no mean antagonist. The natives trap the hyæna, and take pleasure in mocking and teasing the prisoner prior to despatching him.

The Chief of the Shilluks is styled the Mek, and is an important individual. His son, a very smart young buck, who had charge of his spear—a particularly good example—would come often into Fashoda, being partly attracted, no doubt, by the gift which usually awaited him. His father's predecessor had proved unamenable to enlightened ideas or to reason, and was deposed in favour of the present chief, who has proved rather more satisfactory. I had the honour of seeing some of his ladies, who were in hospital suffering from an unfortunate indisposition.

As is no uncommon occurrence in Fashoda, the weather was warm, and the little brick palace assigned me was stifling at night. Publicity is not embarrassing there, and one's bedstead outside in the big, open space seemed quite *en règle* and right. True, if the wind blew beyond zephyrs, the dust was somewhat atrocious, and the scent from the *khor* was occasionally vile ; but the coolness made up for all limitations save one : to discover this baffled my ingenuity. Night after night I woke up in misery, but the irritant always evaded the most rigorous search. Morning showed nothing ; the common flea was not, sand-flies were not to be seen. It was some dark speciality of Fashoda, ghostly relics of Abdullah's tortures, left behind to take vengeance by night.

One is not even alone in one's house; a large species of wasp also inhabits it, taking scant notice of mankind unless he provoke. It builds mud dwellings on the walls, and in each cell an egg is deposited. Its chief characteristic is unmitigated pertinacity and perseverance. No matter how often, in safety during the builder's absence, the construction be destroyed, fresh mud is brought from the *khor*, and operations recommenced without symptom of annoyance or surprise.

The lizards, too, are a source of amusement and comfort. The flies of Fashoda are no less a nuisance than elsewhere, and temperature being extreme, likewise is intolerance of them. So one thanks God for the small lizard which comes to the rescue, and so tamely and confidingly meanders in quest of his food. One sits down to read, and the fly makes that impossible. Despite the heat, every inch of exposed skin is wrapped up to avoid him, and a seroot settles down, or wasps and bees utter their menacing note; then blessings are invoked on the wee reptiles who so unhesitatingly capture these torments, and wishes are fervent that they may gather in greater numbers around, to free one from pests and from stains on one's vocabulary!

At a spot on the Mountain Nile I once saw a duel between a bat and a lizard—swiftness of wing versus swiftness of leg. That a bat should consider a lizard his prey, or *vice versa*, seemed unlikely, yet the evolutions performed left no doubt, and were only ended by the entrance of a servant.

In this country the lives of cattle alternate between conditions of plenty and famine. These are nothing if not extreme. 1908 was remarkable in the Sudan for the superfluity of maize, which was left to rot in the fields. At other times or in other places dhurra may be so scarce as to cause famine, requiring the good offices of Government. So, in the wet season, unfortunate is the animal which does not get sleek and fat on the abounding green grass. He requires all his flesh to carry him through the dry season, and at the end he resembles a bag of dry bones. But if the fat kine become scarecrows in these terrible months, how fares it with the lean? They fall lower and lower, dying by inches, becoming the prey of a small but terrible fly, which, as the poor beast rolls on the ground in endeavours to rid himself of it, swarms in great numbers reciprocatingly to the side which comes uppermost. Thus the suffering animal is badgered to death.

Walking down one day to the river, our eyes were directed to a woman approaching us, with a comparative grace and distinction most unusual in this land of unæsthetic form. She carried the usual calabash on her head for her husband, from the waist upward her body was only half veiled by a semi-transparent cloth, and her features and figure were pleasing. My companion remarked, as he passed her, that he thought she must be of the Baggara tribe. Catching the word, she instantly turned, and, as if considerably resenting the implication, said: "Ana mush Baggara; ana Habashi" (I am not Baggara; I am Abyssinian). She was the wife of a soldier, and had been taken in early youth from the neighbourhood of Kassala. Her voice, too, was distinctly an improvement on the hoarse animal utterances of the Arab creature, whom it is difficult sometimes to credit with being human. Even the raw negroid ladies of marshland seemed to approximate sweet femininity more nearly than these.

I determined to cross over to the far island opposite Kodok to try to bag hippo, which were lying at the upstream end some 500 yards away. A walk through the grass on the flat surface might not be disagreeable, and the difficulties encountered were by no means expected.

As the felucca approached the mud shore, two crocodiles, hidden in the grass, silently slipped into the water, and I realized that the nice, soft grass, as it looked from over the river, was cane-like, three-quarters of an inch thick in the stem, meeting well over my head in full strength, and matted and tangled; it would be a formidable obstacle to progress, and the noise of the passage might be considerable. Then, again, it was 1 p.m., and the heat, both direct from the sun, and, almost worse, as the sun was overhead, that also retained and reflected by the grass and transmitted from below, was intense and indescribable. Still, in for a penny in for a pound, and it seemed foolish to turn back. Pushing, climbing, and struggling, falling often with one leg in a hippo's footprint, I burst my way into the centre where hippos wandered at night at their feed, and gave vent to the strange, grunting bellow which reached through the darkness to one's bed on the shore. To be charged in the midst of the tangle would be far too exciting for actual pleasure.

A peep on the shore showed that the unavoidable rustling of grass had done its expected work—presumably, a self-respecting hippo would not go ashore here at midday; they had smelt danger, and had moved from the shallows where they would have afforded a most easy shot. One fronted me halfway over the river, his nostrils and ears above water. He sank dead as a doornail, and the river soon carried him north to be food for expectant Shilluks. Every black head disappeared at the shot, and full half an hour was spent on the grill before a second opportunity occurred. This time the bullet crashed through the skull, the impact causing a noise which sounded to listeners down-wind almost like that of a second report. The strange habit of the hippo, unlike any other animal I know of, is to dive backward. Time after time, while waiting and watching, I was reminded that two can play at that game, for often the upper surface of a long, scaly body in mid-stream could be seen taking stock of position and reckoning chances.

Worse than ever was the quarter of a mile back to the felucca. The heat being overpowering and the exertion killing, I was left far too exhausted to take interest in any subsequent proceedings.

A couple of foreign sportsmen once had, with their servants, a most disagreeable experience on the White Nile. Presumably taking their cue from native hunters, they shot at and wounded a hippo from their small boat. He got cross, and, not being disabled, charged the boat furiously, crunching it in his jaws and sinking it. The occupants fortunately escaped with their rifles, and, according to the story handed on to me, succeeding in mounting one of the small islands of "sudd," cut away in course of the clearing of blocks up the river, which come floating down. So far, so good; but, huddled together, to their dismay the heads of a whole herd of hippo made themselves visible around. Ammunition had mostly gone down with the boat, but fortunately they were not again attacked, and after a long delay succeeded in reaching the bank.

On Lake No—the expanse formed by the junction of the Bahr-el-Ghazal with the Mountain Nile, where the latter comes in from the south to flow eastward awhile as the head of the White Nile—the hippos are particularly savage and numerous, and the natives in their slight canoes are in continual danger of being attacked.

CHAPTER X

THE "CREWE JUNCTION" OF THE NILE

As we steamed southward up-river, a few Shilluk boats were crossing, bringing in the last of their taxes in kind, dhurra being its form.

To Tewfikieh is fifty-five miles, and this space gave occasion some years before for a demonstration of the great powers of endurance a native possesses, and will exhibit when put to it. One of our sailors was a tall, negroid Arab, powerfully built, and known by the name of Sheikh. In most ways a reliable man, he had the failing which so many white brethren succumb to. The neighbourhood of the *suk* at Tewfikieh proved too much for him; there was merissa in plenty, and Sheikh had been weeks up the river with us, even as far as Gondokoro.

So he fell; the steam-whistle called on stupefied ears, and "bukra" (to-morrow) appealed more to him than his sense of the urgency of the summons. So after an hour had been spent by the steamer battling with the breeze, and it had just succeeded in breaking away from the bank, a black figure, wildly gesticulating, fled along on the opposite bank, shedding white garments as he ran, and rolling them up, with many verbal instructions, borne down faint on the breeze, to the *reis*. It was no use; once free of the shore, making way in the teeth of the wind, the steamer would not stop for the delinquent, and the last visible of poor Sheikh was a lonely white point in the distance, plodding silently on.

At Kodok next day, some time before leaving after the usual short stay of the steamer, I went on to the upper deck, and there saw a familiar figure, recumbent in deep sleep. It was Sheikh, who in the twenty-four hours had travelled on foot the whole distance, much of it during the night, and had finished his journey of fifty-five miles by swimming the river.

He had the grace, this good-natured giant, to look rather sheepish and small when I laughed at him, and thenceforth lost no opportunity of atonement for his error, even fishing for a crocodile which I had shot, and had got into waist-deep water, by wading in to search with his legs!

The banks grew more and more populous as we progressed, mainly on the west bank; little groups stood at the *meshras* (landing-places), men strode along the banks, and black nippers tended herds of slowly grazing cattle. Here and there on the edge of far-distant bush could be seen the forms of shy antelope, and conical hut roofs dotted the skyline.

On either side of the steamer we were accompanied by double-decked sandals, or barges, carrying a consignment of women-folk from Kodok to Tewfikieh, where their husbands, the soldiers, awaited them. The crowd was enormous; one could scarcely have picked one's way through them. When it comes to remembrance what a hullabaloo even two native women create when they talk, the resultant from scores comes within measurable distance of rivalling the volume of sound produced in the tea-room of a ladies' club in London. It was preferable to the latter, being in the open air, but at night proved disturbing, and stern measures had to be taken.

Some of the women were girls of Tolodi, a locality some days west of Kodok, where a rising took place in 1906, resulting in the murder of the Egyptian Mamur who was in charge, and of a number of his soldiers.

The colour of these young women much resembled the even, blacklead tint noticeable in the Basuto in South Africa, and stood in pleasant contrast to the somewhat dirty chocolate of the Arabs.

Where the country is so consistently flat, a slight rise comes as an agreeable variety, and when crowned with thick-foliaged trees Elysium seems to be reached. Amongst the prettiest spots on the river was one such locality, when a large grove of palms was divided in two by a small number of huts. It is noticeable in the Sudan that the native does not cultivate trees round his habitation. His villages are often a collection of beehives stuck on a treeless plain, and the idea of having a tree near one's front-door to provide shade does not seem to specially appeal to them. Its absence may aid them in keeping free from mosquitoes.

In this instance it was different, and palm-groves not being too common, the fruit and the leaves, from which cordage is made, may have been the attraction. It was a quite pretty sight—the hay-coloured roofs and dull red of the huts, amongst the green of the tall, handsome palms. The little girls were strolling down to the river with their water-pots, splashing and shrieking in the water; lithe, naked men laboured at building a hut, or sat smoking their long pipes at ease, while the women had a certain dignity and ease of carriage which gave grace even to the patchy oxskin slung over one shoulder.

The population has increased enormously even in the last two or three years. In the old days few *tukls* (huts) would have been seen by the side of the river; pheasants would just as securely rest by the lair of the fox. But now an almost continuous line of these buildings exists for scores of miles, and the cattle seem innumerable, which the ravages of cattle disease in 1908 have not seriously affected.

At a spot by name Lul, where the ground rises considerably higher and farther away from the river than usual, was a long, low building of brick, a mound, and a cross, marking the Austrian Jesuit Mission. "Shadoofs" from the river sent their water some hundreds of yards, and a fever-worn brother stood on the shore. Yet better here is their lot than that of the self-sacrificing Father Knoblecher, who in the barbarous days of 1848 penetrated far up the Mountain Nile to Kenisa (Church), or Heiligen Kreuz, only six degrees above the equator. There in the midst of the most desolate morasses and forest, where nature as well as man was vile, where daily existence could have been nothing short of torture, he and his brethren spent their days and lost their lives on a mere patch of ground above water, amongst scattered members of a degraded race. When I was there, little if anything remained to mark the post. One large tree with thick, pendulous pods hung over the water; a tangle of small growth matted the eminence which held the bones of some seventy victims. There is romance in this desolate spot; it is still *heilig*—gone is the earthly, remaining the spirit, and one may believe that, in vain as it may have appeared at the time, the effort was not entirely wasted.

Onward to the high bank of Tewfikieh, crowned again by the rustling shade of the broad-leafed palm, where the steamers of the Irrigation Department and of the monthly Gondokoro service lie alongside, and the long spars of ghayassas tower high in the air. The last station before the three great routes branch off to the east, south, and west, it may well deserve the name of the "Crewe Junction" of the Nile.

Providence orders a certain fitness in the materials which are placed ready to hand for the use of mankind, and of these the natives avail themselves. The mud which the Arabs employ for their huts is fairly resistent of heat; bricks are made for the white man, being dried in the sun. In the dry season grass walls have their advantages, letting the breezes pass through; but summer brings tropical rain, and thatched roofs often leak—in fact, it is often difficult to find a dry spot in a hut at these times. Civilization brought with it corrugated iron, with a lining of wood for its roofs. It did not stop there, but constructed whole houses and stables, which roasted their inmates. Of all the contrivances for the discomfort of members of the animal kingdom, perhaps the earliest designs of the tin house adopted in the Sudan were the worst in a broiling hot climate, and men have often resumed life in their huts as a matter of preference. Double roofs are sometimes arranged, but the eaves cannot be left open to allow of a current of air, on account of the thousands of bats which would take refuge thereunder. Broad verandahs and much greater intramural air-spaces are now provided, with quite satisfactory results.

Considering the discomforts and dangers under which pioneers labour, and the devotion they show in performance of duties, one may well urge that their housing be made a matter of paramount consideration. And seeing what was accomplished years ago by Belgium in the Lado Enclave—reached, not by the waterway, but across continent—one falls to considering why the Sudan is behind. Tightness of money there is, but vast sums are spent at Khartoum, as in the building of an enormous embankment, a tithe of the cost of which might well mean the saving of lives up the country if expended in that direction. Still, yearly improvement is being made in this matter under skilled direction, and it is to be hoped that not a long time will elapse before all the important stations are provided with healthy and satisfactory housing.

Tewfikieh was founded by Baker, and has consistently, but perhaps not altogether wisely, been continued as a station for troops. Doubtless the great explorer was attracted by the high bank and the grove of palm-trees, but it has the fatal defect of having swamps quite adjacent. There are few places which have not, however, and so much money has been spent of recent years in buildings that probably, unless heroic measures be taken, the choice will be perpetuated. The adjacent irrigation base is more fortunately situated.

Many Shilluks stroll around, and one or two young men come up to enter into conversation. They are amiable, but incoherent, their Arabic being faulty, and it is to be feared that they have become accustomed to see the tourists who travel from Khartoum to Gondokoro and back, and find that an occasional garush or piastre may be earned by their smiles. The value of money is being learnt by the river-side, and the unconsciousness of nudity has departed. The purchasing power of coin is already applied by the weak ones to merissa, and the blessings of civilization develop.

There is always a certain degree of regret felt when a people emerge from a primitive state and take on the beginnings of our so-called culture. If they are savage and crude, they are children of Nature, and more or less honest about it. Imperfect as are results in our own cases, we too often show them that primeval man is still in us, and the incongruities which are the effect of a struggle between right and wrong, or a falling short of ideals, may appear to them simply as proof of pretence. They learn that life becomes greatly more complicated, its conditions being more onerous, and, not possessing the expert acquaintance which our long custom and intelligence brings of their employment, they tend to get muddled and lost, which involves the moral chaos which has been remarked on times without number.

Yet these smart young bucks, done up in beads, ostrich feathers, and paint, with marvellous constructions of their hair and fanciful adornments, had the advantage of pleasant manners, and one deemed it necessary to apologize for the fact that he had business elsewhere, and must leave me, by making the statement, "Ana rua" (I am going). Probably the less refined savage would simply have *gone*, without the politeness of such explanation. Verily, here in Shilluk-land the suffragette might well turn the tables, and say: "Vanity, thy name is man."

The inhabitants of Tewfikieh would deem that one of the principal features of the place had been scurvily treated if mention were not made of the two elephant skulls which stand by the door of the officers' mess. One will gravely give you the history that they are relics of Baker's prowess in the days of his sojourn with big-bore muzzle-loaders, and then proceed to smile at you for falling a victim to fable; another will heartily vouch for its accuracy. What can the poor visitor do in such turmoil of testimony? Perhaps the balance lies in favour of the truth of the statement, as they are certainly old; Baker was a great elephant shot, was at Tewfikieh, there are no witnesses against him and no other claimant.

The influence of the "sudd" country to the south seemed to be made evident here, for the temperature was steamy and hot to a degree—102 degrees in the shade. Little relief came at night, and the settlement looked like a miniature Cowes from the river, owing to the unusual number of nuggars and steamboats crowding the bank, their multitudinous lights mingling with those on the shore.

Only a few miles separate us from the point where the Sobat, the most southern of the Abyssinian rivers (save the less important Asua), debouches into the Nile, and it marks the most southerly point of the great section styled the Bahr-el-Abiad (White River). The Sobat meets the joint streams of the Bahr-el-Gebel (Mountain River) and the Bahr-el-Ghazal coming in from the west, almost face to face, the course then being deflected northwards.

At the junction is the site of a late Dervish fort, commanding the three waterways. It had been hoped that the Sobat would develop into the most important route into Abyssinia. Steamers ply for a long distance along its course, and a trade centre has been leased by the Sudan Government at Gambela, in Abyssinian territory. But navigation in the upper reaches is too uncertain for full use, and there is some disappointment.

Some few miles up the river is the American Mission among the Shilluks, and far away up is the spot where poor General Gatacre died, lonely and unattended. There is something peculiarly striking in the fact that his grave should be made at so isolated a spot in the land which his great energies aided in rescuing.

It is perhaps appropriate at this point to refer roughly to the general scheme of the Nile and its tributaries in reference to the life-giving flood which renders Egypt a land of prosperity rather than desert. But for its tributaries cultivation would be confined to the narrowest limits, for the amount of effluent from the stream south of the Sobat varies but little the whole round of the year, on account of the low-lying marshes of enormous extent which a slight rise of the water spills into.

This circumstance affects the river almost from its source, for the excess of Victoria Nyanza in the summer is soaked up in marshes on the Victoria Nile, while that of Lake Albert is disposed of in the regions of "sudd" on the Mountain Nile south of Lake No. The Bahr-el-Ghazal suffers similarly. It is in the direction of controlling this treasure that improvement is coming; but though schemes of dams and canals are being considered, the regulation necessary to irrigation is yet in its infancy, and meanwhile the Sudan of necessity more or less starves.

The dredging of the channel through the Zeraf is already in progress, and it is hoped that the improved carrying capacity of the channel, supplemented eventually by a dam retaining the surplus waters of Lake Albert, will supply the needs of Egypt; this leaves the Blue Nile free for the purposes of the Sudan, which will naturally be directed to the Ghezireh, lying between the Blue and the White rivers, and long known for its productiveness. The latter part of the scheme, in its fullest development, depends on problems which have yet to be solved, but in the meantime there is ample scope for effort in the initial stages of the work.

The three main contributing rivers are the Atbara, Blue Nile, and Sobat, in their order from north to south, and all rise in the hills of Abyssinia. The Atbara, being nearer the mouth, naturally wins the race, and its flood comes down first; then comes the Blue Nile, but its waters are held up by the force of the earlier torrent, and, backing into the more upstream bed, fill it and form a natural reservoir. Precisely the same occurs as between the Blue Nile and the Sobat, so that not till the Atbara commences to slacken does the Blue Nile come fully into play, and only after the latter has finished its turn does the Sobat come in. There is thus a natural regulation and prolongation of supply, which is artificially augmented by the great dam at Assuan.

The explanations of the ancients respecting the rise and fall of the Nile are interesting and amusing.

For eighty miles or so from the most southerly point of the White Nile, the river, now over 500 miles to the south of Khartoum, flows almost due east from the west, as the Nasamonians of Herodotus reported, and at Lake No the Mountain Nile joins from the south at right angles. There is thus, as between the White Nile and the Mountain Nile, a rectangular shoulder, across which a branch or short-cut of the river runs diagonally. This is the Bahr-el-Zeraf, or Giraffe River, very well named, for many of these creatures were seen in the course of the next few days.

The entrance to the Zeraf was most abrupt. From the great waters of the wide Nile one's eyes suddenly fell on grassy plains on either side of the steamer, and almost touching the sandals alongside. The effect produced was as if we were sailing across the dry land. On our left were the far-away Gebels Zeraf, five in number, blue in the shimmering atmosphere. All around them was grass-covered plain, with scarcely a tree to be seen.

To the right a strange object appeared, a lump in the distant high grass, and it moved. At one moment it seemed to dodge hither, slowly yet steadily; then it altered its course and travelled elsewhere, growing steadily larger as it apparently traversed the plain. It was only a steamer, on the hidden main river, which ran at an angle with the Zeraf, and gave the peculiar effect we ourselves would present on our invisible waterway. Far beyond her was the great Mountain Nile, the stream directed from the south once again on the other side of Lake No.

It was on its shores in this latitude that I once counted seventy-five elephants in one evening, some still bathing and drinking in the unreachable swamp, perhaps not 500 yards from the boat. Others streamed across the vast expanse—old bulls with mighty tusks gleaming white in the sun, cows with their little ones following, making lines of slow-moving black objects. One strange effect is shown. A far-distant animal at an instant expands to double his size, and shrinks as quickly again; it is not due to exaltation on the part of the observer, but to the elephant's back being toward one, and his ears being occasionally held at right angles! The consequent increase in width is enormous. The white skulls of elephants are sometimes seen as we pass the spots where their owners have fallen to somebody's rifle.

On the ghayassa we are towing are some 30 tons of dhurra, looking for all the world like coarse gravelly sand. It is to prove useful in getting into friendly touch with the Nuer tribes up the river, who had until very recently declined to submit themselves to Government rule, and had from early days been hostile and suspicious of Europeans. There was particular interest, therefore, in going among a people so fresh to intercourse with civilization.

In the stern of the boat is the little cockpit where poor withered old Mary Ann, stripped to the waist, drudges at her patient slavery. She is cook for the sailors, and was doubtless a slave in her time. Bending on her knees, with a flat stone before her, spitting on her hands, she grinds the moistened dhurra on it with a smaller stone, backwards and forwards, backwards and forwards, till one wearies with the ceaseless movement. Only once does she stop, to project overboard with remarkable accuracy and force a mouthful of saliva.

Later on she sits beside an iron plate, well greased with rancid fat or butter, over her wood fire ; a gourdful of her porridge-like flour is placed on the plate, spread out till it forms a thin circular wafer some 16 inches across, and covered by a basket it bakes quickly into the *kisra*, or unleavened bread, of the East. When meat is on hand she cooks stew in the great iron pot, and her work is unceasing. Often one wakes in the night to hear the familiar scrub, scrub, in the darkness—Mary Ann grinding her corn in the cool of the night.

Beside her may be seen an Arab who holds a gourd high in the air, so that whole, uncrushed grain may pour into his cooking-pot for boiling with soup, the wind carrying dust away in its fall. This is another method of preparing the grain for purposes of food, and, being a man, he would starve rather than do feminine work at the grindstone.

On the sandal was an old Nuer lady, who had been living in a state of high culture at Kodok, having learned to wear clothes as an Arab. She was taking an opportunity, eagerly sought after, of visiting her relatives on the Zeraf. By her side was a man of ineffable ugliness, some of his front-teeth knocked out and others protruding, naked and black, his tufty hair red with cowdung and clay, projecting backward and upward.

Berberi and Sudani servants, with the amphibious *bahari* of the First Cataract, the tall, yellow, and slow Egyptian soldiers of our escort, a Greek engineer, and the Englishmen, made up a Noah's Ark in the way of mankind.

Game is very plentiful here, but there was little opportunity under the circumstances of the journey to bag any; moreover, there was an unusual amount of water in the country for this time of year, which rendered it unnecessary for game to come actually to the river.

Here were the handsome, cobby waterbuck, with

heads far finer than I had seen on the Dinder; one stood, unmoved by the sight of the steamer, on an islet in the midst of a swamp not far from the bank. Scattered over the grassy plains were many of the dark-skinned "white-eared cob," with their white patches on the head and throat, and light bellies. Their sober-hued wives were in numbers.

Seizing an easy opportunity to land where a cob stood in a convenient position, and crouching as I crept under the cover of grass, I eventually peeped through an opening, and, resting a moment, fired as the animal prepared to move off. But the exertion in the full blaze of the sun had made me out of breath, my heart was beating quickly, and the bullet missed its mark. Instead of bolting full tilt, he stopped dead though half covered with grass, and the next shot was successful.

Not far from this spot the engineer told me in his broken English how a British Bimbashi went out after a cob just as I did, and wounded it slightly. It went off into long grass, the Bimbashi following. Those on board the steamer then saw a bit of by-play worth attention. As the Bimbashi moved on, so did another keen hunter; as he stopped, so did the other. A lion was tracking the sportsman in turn, but the unsuspecting man fortunately returned without having been attacked by his unseen antagonist, innocent as he was of all knowledge that he had been in danger from a deadly enemy, and from the other point of view had lost a valuable trophy! The sudden dash of two long, low animals from the water-side in the evening demonstrated that walks abroad are liable to be productive of incident.

Birds became more numerous than I had noticed since Sennaar had been left, but many familiar voices were absent. The great saddle-billed stork (*Ephipporhyncus Senegalensis*) walks in a preoccupied way, searching for frogs and small fish; his enormous bill is orange, vermilion, and black, his wings are sooty, and his breast white with a circular "pom" of orange on it. In Uganda he is prote eted, but here there is less reason for this measure, as he is fairly plentiful, and inhabits districts not much visited by sportsmen or collectors.

Black divers crowd a tree here and there, drying their wings in a quaint posture, for they are extended as if spatchcocked or crucified, standing stiffly nailed out. White cranes slip along with their serpentine necks, their heads and bills being of no greater diameter, and the wee black and white kingfisher hovers busily, with his head bent down at right angles to his body, gazing intently and then dropping plumb.

Old man marabouts still put in an appearance, and the harsh cry of the crested crane makes itself heard. The straw-coloured tuft of this bird with the black velvet behind it makes the distinguishing badge of one Sudanese battalion.

A brown eagle sits on a tree by the river; the

binocular shows clearly his fierce, yellow eye, gazing unblinkingly in the strong light, while the white head and shoulders of the great fish-eagle cause him to be marked from afar. The under-surface of his feet are peculiarly rough, resembling intensified sand-paper, and thus are specially adapted to the grasping of fish.

Over the trees to the eastward are nine slanting projections, each topped by four tiny knobs. They seem stilted and stiff, and stand out well defined in the landscape; these are giraffe, which are seen here in plenty.

Teal appear in great numbers, and form a refreshing change of diet. The sand-banks are often covered with vast crowds of these birds and Egyptian geese resting awhile, showing a forest of necks, all turned together in the same direction, as is the manner of wild-fowl.

A little mouse-brown bird haunts the edge of the rushes; it rises as the steamer approaches, and appears transformed to a pure white one as it flies a little way along, then disappears into its un-prominent hue again as it settles.

The forest where it touches the winding river is everywhere greatly broken down by elephants; a walk through thick bush showed hundreds of acres which had so suffered. No very fresh elephant spoor was visible, but that of antelope and lion was in plenty, and the remains of a kill demonstrated the recent visit of the latter. Quite recently I had met an Austrian gentleman who

TREES BROKEN BY ELEPHANTS: BELAL AND FARAGALLAH.

NUER PADDLING CANOE.

To face page 208.

had wounded two lions from his boat lower down on this river.

The Bahr-el-Zeraf was closed to those travelling under ordinary conditions, owing to the fact that the Nuers had only recently been brought into touch with the Government, an important expedition to the chief village having just been accomplished. A few specially favoured sportsmen had permission to go some way up the river, but, being generally at the mercy of the wind, they did not get beyond the confines of the great, treeless, open swamp-land which forms the middle section of the river.

An armed expedition a considerable time before had had a hostile reception, but it was without doubt due to the lying tactics of the irresponsible Dinkas of the Khor Filus, which opens into the Sobat east of the Zeraf, who are always on raiding terms with their Nuer relatives. They undoubtedly spread reports that the pacific expedition was coming in reality to eat the Nuers up!

So the interesting and, parenthetically, intensely trying journey into the interior of swamp-land, where food and potable water were scarce indeed, to the settlement which was the common Mecca of the Dinkas and Nuers, had had important effects in disarming suspicion, which were made apparent to me very shortly afterwards.

The Nuers inhabiting the confines of the White River between the Sobat and Lake No had naturally had some little intercourse with Europeans. Even

Werne in 1840 had dealings with them, finding the men very shy, however, in contradistinction to the women's loquacity; but in the heart of their country, which we had now penetrated, this had been practically nil. The passage of an irrigation steamer had generally been the sign for the natives to disappear, and it was some way to the south, among the Twi Dinkas, that Mr. Grogan had the most unpleasant experience of his pioneer journey from the Cape to Cairo, his caravan being attacked.

Small wonder that the poor wretches were nervous. The whole history of Africa reeks with blood and oppression, and these negroid tribes had suffered since the birth of history from the wickedest actions of mankind.

It is difficult to comprehend the scheme of life which creates vast numbers of human beings for destruction by murder. That disease should come fortuitously to keep numbers in check is within human understanding, but not even the doctrine of survival of the fittest appears to entirely explain the provision of a race which has existed, not merely for the purpose of supplying slaves, but apparently for periodically being almost annihilated by fellow human beings, including each other.

It was on the Zeraf that Ali Wad Rahma had a large slave-station, and was interfered with by Baker on his memorable journey in 1870 and onwards, to suppress the slave trade and annex the Equatorial Provinces to Egypt. The slight eminence which was its site is still visible.

The Zeraf at this period was a mass of agglomerated "sudd" in its upper reaches, and only the superhuman exertions of Baker and his engineers enabled him to cut a way for his following of 1,600 men through the matted vegetation to the White Nile. The site of "Baker's Passage" is still known.

CHAPTER XI

THE TASK OF ADMINISTRATION

THE executive government of those parts of the British Empire under direct rule is held in marvellously few hands, and it often happens that the more remote and dangerous the districts, the fewer seem to be the men who control and develop.

Whole territories are under the sway of single individuals; matters affecting great expanses and thousands of people are decided by solitary men, who inherently and almost unconsciously personify the supremacy of white over black, and through whom the beneficent influences of enlightenment spread to the ignorant masses they govern.

Most of their work is done in the darkness which distance and official obligation impose; the hardships they undergo, the dangers that threaten, the difficulties they conquer, only come to the light of publicity by some fortuitous circumstance, or are negatively evidenced by a condition of peace and well-being where once was rebellion or anarchy. Yet their work goes silently onward; it is commonly taken as just all that should be expected, and the great British public is too absorbed in its games of football or politics to concern itself much with details of the life and tasks of its workers in the remote quarters of the Empire. Justly appreciated only by the few who have seen and know, or by those who spare time to think and realize, held by comrades as those who, in common with all of them, just do their duty, they pass their lives in strenuous toil or lonely responsibility, and return—if they ever return—to a mother-land which only half knows what she owes them.

To this the Sudan proves no exception. Perhaps no division of the world possesses a greater proportion of men imbued with the instinct of government, whose life every day is confronted with problems so entirely foreign to conditions arising at home, yet whose adaptability of mind enables them to suit actions to circumstances, which often are puzzling, and sometimes almost incomprehensible.

Distances are very great; travel in the interior of the more remote districts, where trouble may most easily occur, is difficult; and personal knowledge on the part of those who govern, or who influence government, is of supremest importance. Moreover, it cannot be too strongly urged that continuity of general policy is to be aimed at if the greatest degree of success is to be attained, and to a considerable extent—though it is not always possible—this renders advisable a similar continuity in personnel.

Probably this policy could be carried out to a considerably greater extent than it is, but it is to be remembered that in a malarial climate it is unfair to a man, whatever his wishes, to continue his sojourn too long in a country prejudicial to health. Yet it is strange that a highly malarial country provides the most important exception to this principle—that of the Upper Nile province, which has been administered by one Governor for no less a period than eight consecutive years. It is the cumulative effect of a broad continuity of administration, and, as far as may be, the retention of those who direct it, or selection of successors of experience and sympathy, which is eventually bound to meet with the greatest measure of success.

In connection with this lies the danger of over-centralization, and since the construction of the telegraph-line the tendency has been for this to become increasingly possible. A competent ruler is best left to his own methods within limits of reason, for in all distant and overhead government there is a liability to interference in detail which diverts the energies and attention of the responsible actor, who, after all, is in the best position to judge facts, and is most directly interested in the advance of his work. This has been exhibited times without number in past years as between Downing Street and our Colonies, though latterly a highly instructive example has been afforded by the bowing of the British Parliament to the wishes of collective South Africa in respect of the elimination of native suffrage—a provision not generally sympathized with in England, and in many quarters cordially disapproved of.

There is, of course, the other side of the shield. A person intensely absorbed in the pursuit of ideal or the application of a principle may give insufficient weight to other influences, and may be led to lose consciousness of the diagonal of the parallelogram of forces. But if this be the case, he will inevitably be faced with results which cannot long be ignored.

The general principle in dealing with the raw negroid races has been firstly to get into touch with them along the more easily accessible routes, to trade with them in order to demonstrate honesty of purpose, to exhaust the resources of patience and tact before falling back on the employment of power. Moral influence against robbery and raids comes next, and so long as belief that a power in the background exists, it is wonderful what results may be attained. Then comes the matter of taxation, and the trouble begins, when firmness and discretion are again brought into play.

After all, the taming of wild man runs on much the same lines as that of wild horses. The horse first has to be caught; the negroid first has to be met in the person of the Chief—not always a matter of ease, suspicion and contemptuous defiance being not seldom exhibited. The initial stages of "breaking"—in a philanthropic sense—may be seen in every variety in the Upper Nile province. The saddle has been placed in position in instances, but it is doubtful whether, despite all the years of sympathetic tact and administrative ability displayed by the administrator, his lieutenants, and others, any day may not see it kicked off for the time. It would be merely an incident in the process of regulation, serious enough in the case of a powerful tribe, and disappointing as a break in the success of the first principles of the policy which has been carried out so remarkably, and with but slight interruption, for fully eight years.

Still, appreciation of power is the controlling influence at the back of every native mind, and the following words, written by me of the Matabele in 1895, apply with little modification and with equal strength to the blacks of the Sudan:

"It may safely be said that, as a native cannot well appreciate a power of which he has not been made practically aware, and that as a general rule the only argument which he recognizes as satisfactory and finally convincing is 'brute force,' whenever he becomes actively demonstrative of his contempt for the power he knows not, or for the justice of its rule, he should once and for all, firmly yet fairly, be made to thoroughly appreciate it by means of an armed force sufficiently strong to render an engagement a well-assured victory. It is surely wiser and kinder, to say nothing as to cost, for any mistaken ideas to be dispelled promptly whenever there are signs that they will lead to trouble, than to let their results devèlop until they become dangerous, and maybe fatal.

"The idea held by humanitarians in England,

that such a people as the Matabele can, in the early days of deliverance from barbarous and despotic rule, be ruled entirely by loving-kindness, or by the slow method of law as at home, and that summary and stern dealing with them, even under the most strained circumstances, is reprehensible, is the idea of one who sleeps thousands of miles away, undisturbed by dreams of assault and murder by fierce and naked savages, and who is forgetful of the fact that cruelty and savagery require in justice the strong, resolute hand. These men, and the methods of ruling them, are not to be judged from a European standpoint; appeal to right and justice would in general be pure futility; a nation of butchers, steeped for generations in the blood of their weaker brethren, their only master is a perception of moral and physical superiority, and where this is the case, humanitarian principles, instead of dictating a milder course, in reality impose the sternest treatment."

It is seldom in the breaking of a broncho that lasso or spur is not at some stage required. Generally the use of the former is the introduction to the process. The Government of this province has gone much farther than this in its dealings with the wild negroid, and has exerted remarkable influence with so small a display of force as to be practically nothing at all.

The great obstacles encountered are the impassability of the countries, and the difficulty of persuading the mass of the natives of honest intentions. To the negroids the white face of to-day is the face of the Turk or Egyptian of pre-Mahdi days, and they argue: "Why should the passing away of the Mahdi make the camelopard change his spots?" Following this reasoning, every white man is still called a "Turk." To disabuse them of this impression has been a first object.

It will be seen how mischievous may be the slightest mistake in policy or action, and how small a point may be taken as confirmation of beliefs, with far-reaching results. Add to this the example given to riverain tribes by those resident in districts inland which are impenetrable at present by any important armed force. The riverain black points to the fact that taxes are not collected from his neighbours inland, and argues that if the "Turk" be not strong enough to compel their compliance, then why should he pay his? And, moreover, if he be not oppressed by his ruler, until he has felt the strong hand he is inclined to think that kindness and persuasion are mere indications that government is weak, and can either be fooled or defied.

Visits by the chiefs to Kodok, and even Khartoum, have been encouraged, but have been rare, and it is feared that the travellers on their return are not always received with credulity. Probably the more intelligent chiefs and some of the elder men exhibit more comprehension, but, as with the Zulus, the young bloods often carry the day. In the case of a successful visit to Machar Diu, now the Sheikh of Gaweir, he was persuaded to assent to return to headquarters with the expedition; but when a movement was made to depart, he was promptly surrounded by the young men, who detained him by force, fearing they never would see their virile leader again.

In many instances it is observable that the women exercise no mean voice in affairs, mostly in favour of preserving the *status quo*, and antagonistic to progress.

The story of the race hatred between the Dinkas and Nuers is worthy of being recorded. Probably about the year 1870 a Nuer named Amer fell out with the rest of his tribe, and in revenge enlisted the assistance of the slave-raider Achmet Nasser, whose memory is perpetuated by the name of the post which he founded and retired to on the Sobat.

Amer guided the slavers to the home of his own tribe, with the result that his people disappeared from the face of the earth, saving those who were taken as slaves. The party then crossed to the east bank of the province of Gaweir, which is the farthest upstream Nuer district on the Zeraf, and marked the extreme limit of my journey. Amer exhibited all the characteristics of the renegade, and excelled the Arabs in cruelty. The people of Gaweir were invited to a conference, enticed into a zariba, which was set on fire, and many perished miserably.

On Nasser's retirement to the Sobat, the son of Amer emulated his father's behaviour, and attached himself to Ali Wad Rahma, whose *dem*, or fort, is still visible. The Nuers endeavoured to enlist the sympathies of the Khor Filus Dinkas against the slavers, but they were definitely refused.

The next event was an expedition by Nuer Amer and the slavers to the district of Lak, on the White Nile side, which was decimated and destroyed; and in the course of many raids on Gaweir a woman was captured who was the mother of the late Sheikh Diu. Desperate feuds ensued, and eventually Diu assumed the dual personality called *kugoor*, one side of which is something external to the human personality, supernatural and mystical. Diu was in reality the name of the mystical familiar of this Sheikh, whose own name (laid aside) was Deng Lakar.

The Arabs then succeeded in turning the indifference of the Dinkas into active resistance, and with Nuer Amer once again they succeeded in imposing the payment of tribute on Diu, who was eventually pressed beyond bounds of endurance on a favourite black-and-white bull being demanded. He refused, and, fruitlessly appealing once more to the Dinkas, gathered his spearmen and irresistibly drove the former north to the Khor Filus, all save a remnant of the Ol tribe, which fled to the protection of the Twi Dinkas farther south.

The arrival of British power put an end to Arab interference, but the Ol and the Khor Filus Dinkas have consistently followed the cunning, thieving habits which their ancestor Deng Dit condemned them to. This naturally results in reprisals being made by the Nuers, and Government has to step in to arrange matters.

At the time of my arrival on the Zeraf, the old man Diu had just been visited by the Governor and his Inspector, with the smallest of following. There is much meaning involved in these words. Consistently hostile as the Nuers had been, it was of immense importance from an economic, as distinguished from a political, standpoint to establish relations which would insure safety for the members and work of the Irrigation Department and the telegraph-wire to the Southern Sudan. The situation might have been met by force of arms, the employment of which would have been highly undesirable. Therefore this successful visit to Diu, the first occasion on which he had met his white neighbours, was the vindication of a policy which has secured unhindered opportunity and immunity from danger ever since. A description of the journey makes instructive reading. Owing to the unusual quantity of water, it proved impossible to effect a landing at all at any reasonable distance up-river; the downstream Sheikhs pronounced all landing-places impossible, and the friendly Sheikh Toi Thif was unable to join the expedition at all. Returning almost to the mouth of the Zeraf, an inland route of the most trying description was taken. True it is that ignorance of locality and apprehension as to potable water add great mental trials to the severity of a march, and the six days' journey south to Luang Deng, the joint Mecca of Nuers and Dinkas, was a vivid example of this.

Awoi was reached next afternoon, after two hours' struggle through mud; and at a *morah* (cattle kraal), on the eighth day from the start, an influential Sheikh, a relative of Diu, put in an appearance. This gentleman had apparently been sent to report on the strangers, and affected an attitude of scornful indifference—in fact, it suggested contempt for the small party of men who presumed to enter the country of Diu. His people naturally followed his lead, particularly as he also had the repute of being *kugoor*.

So the next day, while sitting with Belal, the interpreter, and making belittling comments on the "Turks," he was suddenly struck in the eye by the flash of intense light reflected from a mirror held in the hand of the object of his derision. He faltered and flinched, trying to show no distress as the brilliancy blinded him. His disparaging remarks ceased, and he endured it as long as he could; but, after all, he was only human. His head fell from the glare, and, recovering himself after a moment, he rushed up to his tormentor, sang and yelled incantations in front of him, then shook hands in an ecstasy of admiration and fervour. Speaking in Nuer equivalent, he cried that the white man had proved himself greater *kugoor* than he, and that surely he carried a piece of his god in his pocket!

Thenceforth, as a matter of policy, he was submitted to treatment similar to that which he had

A GATHERING ON THE ZERAF.

To face

meted out to the visitors, and was waved to the background as of little account. He followed the party with the submission of a puppy chastized, and with much loss of prestige in the eyes of his people.

A party of Dinkas was passed, who called to the Sudanese police not to proceed with the "Turks," and to let them go forward alone to their fate; but loyalty and knowledge prevailed.

A grove of trees was the mark to be made for, and the white men strode forward alone. A sound of voices in unison fell on the air, firstly a phrase in the shrillest falsetto, then the deep chant of bass voices. It was the war-song of the Nuers, and as distance decreased the volume of sound was enhanced, the savage voices bursting in full force on their ears when they had traversed the belt of finely-grown trees and saw masses of fully-armed warriors at rest round a pool. The sight was impressive, but Diu was not there. With native suspicion, he awaited the report of his deputies. The spot was quite charming and picturesque, well shaded, and cool to the jaded travellers, and the arrival of the Sheikh, attended by numerous nymphs, was almost dramatic. The arrangement was peculiar, for during the interviews, which spread over two days, he was backed by a semicircle of women, the explanation of this, perhaps, being that he was thus protected from eavesdropping on the part of the men of the tribe. The disposition shown was quite friendly on the pacific intentions of Government being made known.

The return journey by Duk, the headquarters of Diu, twenty-five miles from Awoi, through almost unexplored country north-east to the upper reaches of the Khor Filus, was safely negotiated, and civilization was once again reached after a journey of 270 miles and an absence of twenty-one days.

On a second journey, subsequent to my visit, Diu having died in the meantime, and his son Woll at first succeeding him, the new chief was successfully persuaded to visit Khartoum; and on the return of the party it was found advisable to settle some trouble which had arisen between Machar Diu and Lyam Tu Tiang, then Sheikh of the neighbouring province of Lau. The latter was therefore summoned to meet the representatives of Government, for the dispute to be arranged face to face with Machar, who already had assumed paramount influence. This was highly unpopular with Lyam Tu Tiang, who valued his life, and thought it ran risk of a quick termination if he placed himself in the hands of his neighbour. He reluctantly came, bringing twenty men with him; the case was duly decided, and the arrangement agreed to by both. The Gaweir natives then became excited, and ominous movements took place; so, to ease the situation and divert attention, a war-dance was suggested. But the dance added fuel to fire. A boy came to say that Machar Diu would kill Lyam Tu Tiang and his people, who in despair adopted the attitude customary when all hope has gone—squatting down, with their spears thrust in the ground between their knees, and shaking their hands and arms up and down.

Fortunately, Machar Diu came to the rescue on being appealed to, a bull was presented, and the Sheikhs shook hands with each other in their native fashion. Opportunely, a heavy rainstorm came on, and the dislike of the unclothed savage for this form of water caused them to run helter-skelter for cover.

That night was an anxious one. Time after time in the darkness the weird war-song approached from afar, as fresh parties of Nuers came in to take part. The temper of all was uncertain, and hostile counsels might have prevailed. Lyam Tu Tiang having come in under Government protection, any accident to him or his men would have been considered a breach of faith, with bad results in regard to the people of Lau. Fortunately, a pacific attitude prevailed in the morning, and both Lyam Tu Tiang and the expedition returned safely home.

A further journey was even more fruitful in excitement. Woll was a fine physical specimen, but his character lacked firmness, which was amply supplied in the case of his brother, Machar Diu, who, described by the Governor as a most difficult savage, became chief in practice if not in name. Machar Diu, possessing less worldly knowledge than his father, but considerable intelligence, scouted the idea of interference by the "Turks" when the mission to him was conceived. The two representatives of Government, at first travelling separately, and accompanied in all by six Sudanese soldiers, landed at Kodni, where I had once gone ashore, and marched inland. The matter to be settled was the old story. The Ol Dinkas, from their asylum amongst the Twis, had raided Gaweir and carried off cattle—an insult the proud Machar declined to undergo tamely. With a party of twenty men only, he entered Twi country, burnt a village, and killed several men, retiring then to Gaweir.

It became evident in the early days of the journey, that, while old Diu had been impressed by the previous visit, his people had not. Messages came from Machar Diu, describing in harrowing detail the methods he intended to adopt when he had the white men in his power. "My men will arrive casually, in parties of two or three, until there are sufficient to surround and rush you." This promised an interesting situation, but there could be no drawing back.

On arrival, the Gaweir Nuers commenced to put in an appearance in precisely the manner forewarned by Machar, but increasing in numbers, so that by the time the Sheikh appeared on the scene there were fully 400 armed men in evidence, surrounding the party. The Governor intimated that an essential preliminary to parley was that all of the Nuers should be ranged in a semicircle fronting him, which was immediately acceded to.

The day brought a turn for the better, and, after hours of discussion and argument, Machar Diu was prevailed on to pay "blood-fines" for the killing of the Dinkas, preferring to give 250 pounds of ivory in place of the sixty cattle demanded, and fairly cheerfully contributing six head of cattle as tax. This was naturally considered a most satisfactory outcome of the policy adopted.

Machar Diu proved to be a young man, violently opposed to any control by the Government, although personally showing good-will to his visitors. He was keen and straightforward and showed no deceit, was intellectually far superior to his brethren, virile as a fighting man, and capable of arguing soundly from an intelligent basis. Once convinced of the power of Government, and confidential relations established, he might be a powerful instrument for good; but such a consummation is by no means assured.

Enough has been said to demonstrate the difficulties encountered in attempting to administer such countries as these, and it cannot with any certainty be judged when the limit of pacific policy may not be reached. Even of late the Khor Filus Dinkas have had to receive their first lesson by force, and the turn of Shilluks and Nuers might easily come.

To the authors of this policy this would be a sad day; if they regard it in too circumscribed a light, their work of years might seem to be lost. In reality this is not so, for it is merely the complementary side of the system—the demonstration of strength behind kindness. The spade-work of years may show little apparent result, but, still, it is there, and the hardest part of a nut is the shell.

CHAPTER XII

WHERE LIVES PRIMITIVE MAN

HERE and there we had seen small parties of men making their way along the river-banks, enormously tall and stark-naked. Our Nuer passengers began to evince great interest, and conversations at the top of their voices were frequent. Then three or four ebony figures would be seen hiding shyly behind an ant-hill in the long grass; their *rahats* of shredded palm-leaf proclaimed all but one to be married women, and when they perceived that the steamer had actually passed, the well-known characteristic prevailed over fear, and they mounted the ant-hill the better to see, and to give us the opportunity of appreciating—Eve!

Owing to the heavy barges we were towing, progress had been very slow, and we had not made the way we expected. The spot where it had been decided to cut wood was still some distance away, and a stop had to be made at a place short of it. The felling of timber and taking it on board took the whole of one day, the powerful Egyptian artillerymen working like slaves for the small extra pay which they receive for this work. They are fine, big, powerful men, these conscripts, good-natured and good-looking fellows, who could have escaped their term of military service in a climate so prejudicial to them by a payment of £20.

In the morning we were charging the bank through a belt of long reeds to find a landing-place by the wood, when a confiding waterbuck was seen within a few yards, quite unscared by the ship. Meat was wanted for the men, and my companion determined to shoot it. It moved on to a place where the forest was dense, and, firing somewhat by guess-work, it fell to him at a distance of about 20 yards. Walking up to the animal, he sent back for a knife to bleed it, and for some minutes it lay apparently dead, waited until the hunter had turned his back, then rose to its feet and departed.

Such lack of straightforwardness constituted nothing short of a scandal, and a chase was the only possible course to pursue. However, the gods were in arms for the protection of the buck, and presented themselves in the form of a huge serpent, lying directly in the path. It was a vile, filthy beast, dull fleshy red in colour, and as thick as the arm. Returning with the shot-gun, it was found that the serpent had saved itself by disappearing, and incidentally rescued the waterbuck, for he had got clear away in the interval. As a rule, snakes will make off if disturbed at not too close quarters, unless their refuges be on the other side of the observer. Two pythons killed at Mongalla by a friend were 20 feet long.

This was not the only despitefulness exhibited by the gods of this district. The most interesting and saddening fact revealed itself, that not half an hour before our arrival, perhaps scared away by our noise, the whole river-bank had swarmed with elephants. Their dung was still steaming and their spoor covered acres, while the fresh-broken trees evidenced their destructiveness over a large area. One cannot resist the impression that great numbers of elephants still exist in the Sudan, unless their extreme mobility conduce to an exaggerated appearance of numbers. Who can wish this condition to alter? and who can repress feelings of indignation that slackness of rule, resulting from loss of interest on the part of the Congo State, should have permitted the wholesale destruction of these noble beasts in the Lado Enclave near the termination of the Belgian occupation?

The charm of travel through this country is to see its wild creatures wandering at will, untrammelled by fences, bars, limits, or keepers, over vast tracts of grassland or through the dense forest. Even as our steamer gyrated in the morning in our efforts to effect a landing, a great, tawny giraffe stopped in his lurching walk, and, turning his "Eiffel Tower" of a neck in our direction, calmly surveyed the whirligig beast on the river.

The slow steadiness of the progress of these animals across the plains, prominent as they are even in the far distance, resembles the persistent advance of the tortoise. Deliberation is eminently their characteristic when undisturbed, aided in its effect by their great dimensions.

Two days up the river the vicious seroot flies swarmed to an extent almost unbearable; their presence or absence seemed to be dependent on no particular condition, except, perhaps, the proximity of bush, and they are never seen north of Gebel Ein, 238 miles south of Khartoum, in the dry season.

We had expected to see much game up the river, but were disappointed. The unusual quantity of water in the district for so late a date made it possible for refreshment to be obtained in many places away from the river; but, as "hope springeth eternal in the human breast," we trusted to its making appearance on the other side of the great swampy plain of the middle Zeraf. Here only two specimens were seen the entire day, both poor samples of waterbuck. On the western bank, where a few poor deleb palms eked out a miserable existence with a little straggling undergrowth, my companion had wounded a lion at the water's edge, but he unfortunately got away.

In talking imperfect, halting Arabic in the presence of any of one's own countrymen who are entirely unacquainted with the language, a very wrong impression may easily be gained by them. To instruct the pilot to go "straight ahead, O pilot," astonishingly resembles an objurgation in respect of his eyes; while having most reprehensibly let slip a short pregnant word beginning with *d* on realizing that a shot had gone wide, your shikari will hasten to assure you that you are mistaken, and there *is* no "blood."

A Nuer sent with a message to a village one night reported that on the way he had seen the fresh spoor of a big lion, but the latter took care to steer clear of the boat.

Palms now began to show in the distance, and great was our delight at the thought of getting away from the dreary monotony of the swamp. We headed for a long line of palms stretching in from the west, and made meandering progress towards them for considerable time. But the river was also in league with the gods of the country, and, when within a short distance, one big bend of the stream took us definitely away from the trees. Native *tukls* were now seen in plenty, jutting up against the horizon, four or five miles away from the river, which in the past had been the highway of the Arabs who raided and enslaved their owners.

But before this appearance of human habitation, one of the strange mysteries of the country had light thrown upon it. Often had one asked, when the eye rested on thousands of cranes, egrets, ibis, divers, and the multitudinous varieties of waterbirds, Where do these birds nest, or those of them who do not migrate for the purpose? The answer here was forthcoming in parts of the great sodden plain. At a distance from the stream, in bogland impassable, was a line of trees, thick-growing, but thin and spare individually. Their boughs seemed interlaced, so dense was the growth, and the length of the grove was about 300 yards. The trees appeared to be standing in water, through which reedy grass rose in tufts.

At a distance it was speckled with pure white, grey, and black spots, which a closer acquaintance resolved into myriads of birds roosting or sitting on nests in the trees.

Thick as peas, it might have been expected that pandemonium would have existed, but it was far otherwise. All seemed to have settled down in mutual harmony, secure against every enemy except, doubtless, the snake. Great white birds rested in peace with black divers (there is no colour antipathy here l); grey ones and piebald intermingled at ease. Some waded below, and from far over the marsh sailed others in quest of the room which it seemed hopeless to find. More than one of these rookeries were passed, and it is a misfortune that the damp heat of the climate so damaged the films in the *sanduk iswid* that photographs resulted in failure.

Once again, as we twisted and turned, sometimes almost completing a circle, a long stretch of palm-trees reached out into the swamp. In amongst them were huts, becoming quite numerous, and extending almost down to the river, showing a confidence which would have been rudely shaken in the slave-raiding days. It was pleasant to note that a sense of security was growing up amongst the people.

In mad haste in our path, paddling his palm-trunk canoe for dear life, was a Nuer of splendid proportions. He was endeavouring to reach his village before being overtaken, but for this he could not hope, with all his skill. The wash of the steamer in narrow waters was naturally a matter of concern to the occupant of so easily capsized a craft. The Nuers on board got somewhat excited, as was also invariably the case when figures appeared on ant-hills, roof-tops, or trees, for the purpose of viewing us. The boatman, hugging the bank, was soon relieved of anxiety, and carried a message ashore to his friends.

Judging again from primitive man as he appears to-day, Eve told Adam just the things she ought not to have told him, and omitted some most necessary instructions as to how to behave before ladies, leaving gentlemen out of the question. Mary Jane of the sandal, as distinguished (mainly by a filthy shirt) from Mary Ann of the ghayassa, had occasion, as a somewhat later product of human development, to protest energetically from her kitchen on one side of the stern to Adam alongside her.

The level of the unconscious brute is reached farther south, and is even to be seen among Nuers, where natural functions are performed without notice or movement, or interruption of occupation or conversation.

GROUP OF NUERS.

MARY JANE AND HER KITCHEN.

To face page 234.

Here on board we saw Adam with his first looking-glass—the *ingénu*, the primeval, the crude and unsophisticated! All emotions were exhibited with the frank delight of a maiden at her first ball, and face, attitudes, and ejaculations, demonstrated astonishment and intense self-admiration on the part of a veritable Caliban among Nuers. A negro in front of him, barbarian enough in English eyes, devoted himself, as an unparalleled amusement and recreation, to the instruction of the less tutored savage. His superiority was enormous, his delight and self-conceit unbounded; laughing at the pleasure of the Nuer as he scrutinized the reflection of his somewhat aquiline features, he rolled over with unrestrainable merriment when Adam, on turning to the other side of the looking-glass and expecting to see his own back, looked blank with amazed disappointment.

For harmless occupation and amusement, involving no danger to either party save in the highly unlikely event of success, recreation may take the form of chasing hippopotami in a steamer, always providing that the hippo take the course which the steamer would have pursued were it absent. Narrow though the river be, it has on either side of it grass ramparts which grow in deep water. Among these coarse grass-stems the hippos form their tunnel-like retreats, and the rush for these disturbs the water so much that their course may often be easily observed. Their great heads are all that is seen on first meeting, or, in shallow water, their huge, ungainly bodies. They suddenly awake to the monster coming down on them—a rush, a roll, a plunge, and the water swirls over them. A second later, and a black head rises once more, a fountain of spray may appear as the animal blows, and he makes tracks below the surface once more for his secure hiding-place among the lower stems of the rank green grass, in places where the swamp is wide and provides a retreat impassable for other creatures. Now and again a laugh is raised by the grotesque, pinkish babies recumbent on the half-submerged backs of their ungainly mothers.

Perhaps the most interesting period of the day comes in the evening, when the boat is at rest and the fierce light gives way to the deep-toned, fast-darkening twilight. There is a feeling of restlessness everywhere around, for the air is so still and quiet that one hears all the minutiæ of sound. Small fish rise, rippling the water, and a slight rustling of bush a distance away betokens some creature prospecting for the evening drink. A flight of teal whistles busily up-river, making a sudden sharp sweep away to avoid the but just perceived boat. The hawks and buzzards have gone to rest, and duck and geese are on the move from feeding-places to their chosen dormitories. The human watcher lazily speculates, as he hears a murmur arise by degrees into a high-pitched, continuous *biz-z-z-z*, which will soon drive him to shelter, on their reason for moving, when one place so greatly resembles another.

A tiny, semi-invisible object silently sweeps up on the breeze; it is followed by others, who become multitudinous, filling the air over the river with a mysterious maze of swift-moving shades. Myriads of bats glide flutteringly upstream, as if impelled by a single unseen power, until darkness hides them.

Then come tiny specks of light swinging across the water, chasing sparks from the funnel as if to find unknown brethren, and mingling, separating, winding amongst each other in an interminable, dazing confusion. It is the fireflies' dance, seen at its best in the drear wastes of the Mountain Nile "sudd," where they are the only creatures that show joy in life.

The difficulties of writing are considerable, for the insect world is malicious, much occupied, and entirely selfish. Ants galore career over the table and explore the interior of one's shirt; mosquitoes parade, and cause one to follow their movements with animated interest; winged ants rush everywhere in great haste; hard, armoured beetles dash unavailingly against the wire netting, and lie sprawling outside; grasshoppers and crickets jump in every direction but the one they are facing; and even a grass mantis has become excited and dashes hither and thither, differing from his South African brother by a greater length of wing and celerity of movement. The rest are too numerous and too impatient and restless to mention.

When all is quiet, and even Mary Ann is too sound asleep to snore, a sound of mighty wings comes up the river; the slow, measured swish caused by unseen aerial travellers beats crescendo overhead till they pass away in the mirk.

The deep, restful silence—for to our ears the minor sounds become accustomed—is rudely broken; we are reminded that the night has its uses which are not for men, and for the greater part of the time of darkness we are treated to a concert almost unimaginable in its weirdness.

The voices range from the deepest bass of the hippo to the shrillest treble of the crickets or bell-frogs; the mosquito millions are ceaseless in their note as the sustained drone of the bagpipes. Froggy comes in with varied song in varied *tempi*, hoarse, deep-throated, while an occasional night-bird, careless of discord, sometimes drops in a wild, harsh note. Truly the "Ode to Discord" might well have been inspired here.

The "stars" indeed are the hippos, and the first one speaks from not 20 yards away, for we are tied up at his favourite *meshra*, or landing-place, plainly marked by the passage through the reeds and the deep-trodden track. On the left bank just here, on both banks in many places, they generally lie in the reedy grass during the day, when not basking in the shallows, and venture into the open river and on to their grazing-places at night. Behemoth emerges from his reedy cave and uplifts his head from the water; he takes an enormous breath, with the sound of bubbling wind freed of a sudden, and rushing through a tunnel. Confronted by the strange invader of his midnight haunts, he promptly seeks the cover of the water, only to rise again a short, or even shorter, distance away.

Then comes the song. The first note may either resemble the bellow of a mighty bull or that of an inordinate ass; the second, and those that come after it, deteriorate sadly into the inbreathed snorting of an ill-humoured and deep-toned pig, full of annoyed yet foiled defiance. A hundred yards away one answers to the call; his neighbour opposite replies, and the distance takes up an echoing challenge, which may well, as it seems to the observer, reverberate by its repetition the whole length of the river. There is a vastness in this animal, relic as it is of days when the animal world indeed was vast, which enforces respect, and only becomes ridiculous when it scurries away from its human enemy in undignified haste. The dread "dun cow" killed by Guy, Earl of Warwick, the head of which was dragged in by his men, was forcibly brought to mind by the picture of my Arabs on the Dinder hauling triumphantly into camp the grotesque head of the hippo.

Now, about 150 miles up the Zeraf, it became more of a matter of interest to get into touch with the people. It had been reported that dhurra was extraordinarily scarce, and that famine was imminent, so that a test of the facts was desirable.

Following the wise principle of not pauperizing the people by gifts, the method was adopted of bartering dhurra for oxen, of which there were plenty. Many a time in America an invisible "city" is reached, marked on the railway-line by a name-plate, but with no house to be seen. Much the same was the circumstance here: after a short stay at Ajiung, our farthest point, 144 miles from the mouth, Kodni was halted at, probably the first visit of white men in its history. There was naught on the bank to evince it, not even the American name-plate. But its rights to an individual designation were proved on inspection of the horizon, where some twenty or thirty huts, scattered widely over the country, gave more title to the description of "city" than the American example.

So recently had any kind of relations been established between Government and the important chief Diu — already referred to in the previous chapter as the Sheikh of Gaweir—that some interest was felt in the disposition of folk toward the white men in this more remote section of country. But the fact was well known, though so recent, and touch was immediately, if not freely, affected. I noticed a distinct difference in type and manner between these people and those lower down. They were generally shyer and surly, and did not respond in the manner which was exhibited below. The type of countenance was not so open, and the general disposition less agreeable. This was the first time they had been visited since the old slave-raiding days, and hence their timidity, but it does not account for their character.

Between the river and village stretched a couple of miles of lowland, intersected with swamp every few yards. Messengers were sent out to spread the news of our coming, and all we could do was to wait the result. One or two men eventually turned up, picking their way in a gingerly fashion, and were informed that we would exchange dhurra for oxen. A few more joined their comrades, one of exceptional physique, and eventually some oxen could be seen in the distance threading their way by the track through the slough, and oftentimes sinking from sight in the grass, tugged by thongs round the horns. Some in the distance refused to budge from the higher ground of the village, breaking away and giving the long legs of their owners plenty to do to race round them and turn them toward us. When the bargains were struck, the women turned up in small numbers with baskets; but it was noticeable that the younger ones were carefully kept at home, and only those appeared who were (presumably in their eyes, distinctly in ours) unattractive to look on.

Some filled their baskets with dhurra and took them away on their heads, while others removed it in "dug-outs," which were laboriously paddled or pushed by tortuous channels through the swamp.

In these cases the "dug-outs" were formed out of the trunks of palm-trees, the ends being blocked by hard mud which was constantly being renewed or replastered—frail barks indeed.

A feature of the Nuer country is the ability with which the men build their grass *tukls*, or huts, particularly in the case of the kraals for the cattle. Owing to the plague of mosquitoes and flies in the night, it is essential for all cattle to be shut up within doors. These cattle-huts are of great size, and require considerable skill in construction. The men share this accommodation with the beasts, sleeping on a platform in the centre, on a soft mattress of ash, with a smoky fire of cowdung beneath them. It was apparent that the ash had not a beneficial effect on the skin, which in many cases was excessively coarsened and rough. The front-teeth of the upper jaw were generally knocked out, causing a characteristic protuberance and irregularity of the others.

It is the fashion to mix the milk of the native cow with a small quantity of the animal's urine, which is believed to act as a preservative, and, to my horror, I found that the milk puddings of which I had been partaking, and certainly, though unsuspectingly, noticed a slight unaccustomed flavour in, had been made with this milk.

Among the men there appeared no uniform method of hairdressing—the only dressing indulged in. Fashion evidently decreed no single style. In the case of the Mashonas of Rhodesia much the same conditions were observable, the varieties and complications of patterns being as remarkable as

DINKA CATTLE "MORAH," NEAR BOR.

"MESHRA," HIPPO PITS, AND AJIUNG VILLAGE.

To face page 242.

those of the Fungs and Hamegs, and, indeed, much resembling them.

Some Nuers appeared in the cowdung-tinted tufts described before, others with heads evenly covered with caked ash and urine; some with the same material moulded to a sharpened horn projecting forward, others with an ostrich or crane feather perched on the back of the head.

The heads of the women were invariably clean-shaven. Those who were married wore a coquettish girdle of narrow palm-leaf string or strips, almost efficient for its purpose, and the unmarried girls, of whom two put in an appearance during the last hours of our stay, were emulative of innocent Eve.

Yet in many respects woman in one part of the world resembles woman in others. In some parts Carlton suppers and diamonds are a moving attraction; here it was dhurra and beads that produced symptoms of hankering. The youngest of the party, wearing a skewer of beads through her upper lip, 6 inches long, came quietly forward to me, having decently smoothed down her grass girdle. I retreated on her arrival within a couple of yards while she endeavoured to make a sweet face. She smiled—such a smile! she held her head on one side, with her hand supporting it, to describe how hunger was enfeebling her; she pointed to her mouth, and then to her digestive regions, at which I took fright and incontinently fled.

An aged companion reminded me of Watts's

picture, "The Birth of Experience," where Adam and Eve eat their first oyster. Watts there depicts her as white. The Eve in this instance was black, with burnt ash on her head, and partook of a cayenne-pepper pod or chili in place of an oyster. A small boy, taken by their colour, had a snail-shell full. Eve appeared to have raided him, and for ten minutes after was dancing, bent double, skipping, shaking her head with both hands holding it, rushing backwards and forwards to the river, crying out and spitting consumedly, while Adams of all sizes roared with amusement, and Eves looked concerned. The victim was fortunately good-natured enough, and eventually showed her appreciation of the joke by ending her laments with a shriek of laughter.

Close to the landing-place where we had tied up, were a series of large ant-hills or their counterfeit presentments; inspection demonstrated a large, deep, circular pit in the hard soil, in the immediate vicinity of each. These proved to be traps for the unwary hippo, wandering at night, and in the darkness allowing his fore-feet to step over the brink. He remains in this position helpless, until the morning brings the adversary with spears. Many tusks were in the possession of these villagers, but they are now of little value, since the substitution of porcelain for the manufacture of artificial teeth in Europe.

On the sandy beach near were the white fragments of fresh eggshells in profusion; Nuers standing by demonstrated, rather than informed me, in hoarse, guttural, grunting syllables, that they were crocodile eggs taken from a sand-covered hollow discovered that morning. Prodding the soil with a spear much as a Maori prospects for fossil *kauri gum*, they seek the soft spots of recently disturbed soil in the favourite laying-places of the reptiles. The egg resembles that of a goose, and is filled almost entirely with a glutinous matter so dense as to cause the operation of blowing to be decidedly difficult. I had previously brought a few home to my gamekeeper, who was unable to distinguish them from those of a bird, and whose nerves would have sustained a terrible shock had it been possible to hatch them. Even after experiences with native milk in the Sudan, and on a long trek in Mashonaland, when I ran short of food and was offered a native dish of six-inch hairy caterpillars (preferring to starve for a time), I confess I would decline the delights of a crocodile's egg.

The faces of these savages beggar description. I have studied the physiognomies of Solomon Islanders and of many of the wild men of the Pacific Ocean, but never have I seen such outrageous travesties of the human countenance as these. "Man is only a monkey shaved," sings Gilbert, who would feel almost super-Gilbertian were he here to confess that many a Nuer man immeasurably outrivals the monkey in grotesque hideousness. Yet in some cases it was entirely otherwise, a higher culture from some far-away intermixed blood showing itself in more refined countenances and pleasing expressions.

A feature, strange to our even, well-regulated habits and ideas, of Arab and negro alike, is the ease with which they will subsist and undergo considerable privation on a very small quantity of food, and yet, when an opportunity arises, will calmly sit down and eat incredible quantities at one meal. But it is a land of extremes; in every condition of life the swing of the pendulum is long: the repletion and indigestion—if not worse—which the white man would suffer from in like circumstances have no counterpart here, while he would endure exceeding discomfort and trial had he to subsist in the interim on a few handfuls of dhurra. But in Africa there is no need to provide an excess of bodily heat-productiveness, and the daily pannikin of pony maize which kept Shackleton from perishing in the latter days of his "Farthest South" journey would have kept him at normal temperature here instead of far under.

The readiness to appeal for dhurra, as evidenced by the number of cattle brought up for trade, forced the conclusion that in this quarter at least there was no great scarcity, at least for the time being, this qualification being made on account of the native failing of rarely looking very far ahead of the present. Moreover, the people were generally in fair condition; so while it was obvious, in a country where individual houses are often a

EMBARKING CATTLE AT KWOIN.

DHURRA BEING REMOVED BY CANOE.

Note true colour of skin where wet.

To face page 246.

couple of hundred yards apart, and adjacent villages are correspondingly scattered over wide expanses of morasses, that time was needed to allow people to congregate, there being no evidence of their coming it was deemed inadvisable to prolong delay here. Moreover, the malaria which held the other white man in its grip intensified so seriously as to render a quick journey back to Kodok essential.

Giving news of intended return in a few days' time at a picturesque *meshra* named Kwoin, near a village most mistakenly called "Kool," and leaving sandal and ghayassa behind with instructions to cut wood in the interior, we sped downriver in haste and anxiety.

A few hours from the mouth a great cry was raised by the crew, and expectant faces were excitedly turned to us. "Asud!" called Faragallah, pointing over the plain to the fringe of the bush some three or four hundred yards to the west. How one envies the sight of these men, who, unconcernedly chatting—the busy ones directing the course of the boat, the idle ones napping, or feeding, or dreaming—can spot a live point amongst the confusion of herbage and trees, half covered and distant. With my glass I discovered the slow, lithe walk of the great yellow-brown lion just inside the belt, and moving away.

An opportunity seemed to be before us, but fate had already decreed otherwise; for illness could allow no delay, and communication with the indefatigable *mafatish* had to be effected on one of his fleeting visits to his base down-river. So Leo was left to his meanderings, with high hopes that he would not desert the locality during the day or two which would elapse ere our return.

The sailors had discerned the lioness retiring to the shelter of the grass as her lord strode away. To successfully evict her would entail the firing of the grass from up-wind to drive her from concealment, and expenditure of considerable time.

Faragallah, the Dinka sailor, once had a narrow escape. A lion was seen near the bank, and those on board went ashore and posted themselves in position to shoot it; but it retreated to cover in long grass, and Faragallah proceeded up-wind beyond its supposed position to fire the grass. Mr. Lion had also, however, travelled up-wind, and sat down to await the progress of events. When Faragallah struck his match to fire the grass, Mr. Lion sat up and said "Wouf!" only six feet away. But Faragallah was undismayed by this unexpected announcement, calmly fired the grass, and then bolted off as fast as a huge length of limb would avail him; so did Mr. Lion, in the other direction, and never returned to inquire. This sounds somewhat like a story for children, but as a matter of fact it is one for brave men, as Faragallah showed true grit in waiting, defenceless as he was, to carry out his instructed work.

Two days, unhappily, sufficed for the investigation of this spot by the lions, who had disappeared on our return, leaving only their spoor; and a long search resulted in a total absence of game being made evident, the sole result of the day being a fine example of the African bustard. This large bird trusts to its legs almost as much as to its wings in putting distance between itself and a pursuer, and its wide expanse of brown wing is only unfurled when pressed. Of the turkey kind, its flesh is excellent eating, if somewhat coarse and high-flavoured, and is greatly sought after.

Consequent on this solitary and disappointing success of the chase occurred an incident which demonstrates the difference between the Greek and the Englishman, as it is reflected in the native mind. It has been referred to before that the African Greek has been of extraordinary assistance in the development of the Sudan, by reason of his enterprise, his excessively frugal habits, and a lack of self-respect, which enable him to live much as the native does. But the native by no means admires this trait, and, indeed, looks down on the Greek more or less with contempt.

Still, there are Greeks and Greeks—a distinction which the native mind does not well appreciate; and that the engineer of the boat, despite his limited English, was a distinctly superior person, of some education, appeared no reason to my cook why he should be considered in any different light from the others.

So, on the bustard being delivered to Abid—as chance had it, from the hands of the engineer—my cook misunderstood him, and came to me with the sulkiest countenance, declining to touch the bird on any account. He laid down that he was "No cook for 'Grec'; he cook for Englishman." To expect him to demean his proud position thus was to ask him to do something incompatible with his dignity, and to prostitute his powers. The contempt which he exhibited in his voice and manner was indeed admirable as an expression of one of the emotions. It was evident that a little discretion was required to get round the corner and to soothe ruffled feelings, and, using his own argument, I quietly pointed out that, though the Greek had handed him the bustard, it was my bird, and, even if it had not been, I was to eat some of it, so of course it was a matter of rank impossibility that I could debase myself by eating meat prepared by the cook of a "Grec." Being equally convinced that such a proceeding would be highly improper, he agreed, and retired to his work by no means contented.

On the way down I had seen a huge crocodile, very dark in colour, and distended with eggs, this being the breeding season. It lay in the water among the thick grass, its head being hidden from sight on the bank. I planted a shot in its neck, and as the steamer swirled round in the current, impeding a second shot, after a moment or two of stillness it wriggled feebly into the tangle of reeds, and disappeared to the cries of the sailors saying "Mat" (Dead). The bullet had done its work, and now, on our return, the creature was visible, having crawled into the shallows to die, lying distended and bloated, too far advanced in decomposition to touch.

Close by this spot, too, was the place where a lion had recently been shot by the engineer from the steamer, the wound dividing the throat and tearing the main arteries and veins. Even in his dying and desperate condition he managed to make two or three fierce bounds toward his foe on the steamer, when his rage and determination were all the more impressive because he was voiceless through the destruction of his vocal chords and the choking with blood.

Pelicans are prominent in the swampy reaches of the Middle Zeraf, as much on account of their stupidity as of their size and gliding flight. The recreation of chasing hippo unavoidably turned to that of following pelican.

One appeared in the distance, and endeavoured to swim faster in front of us as we came on. His effort, against the stream, was naturally in vain, and, finding his swimming powers overmatched, he slowly unfolded his far-spreading wings, balanced his huge beak and the deep pouch underneath it, gave himself a slight altitude above the water by strongly patting its surface with his broad webbed feet, then heavily yet easily skimmed low in front of us for a few score of yards, repeating the programme time after time. As we progressed, others were similarly overtaken and joined in the flight from their persistent object of terror, until quite a drove had been accumulated. For two hours the birds failed to devise a means of escape, going directly ahead, though passages opened at intervals on either side. Eventually, when a more obvious opening appeared, by mere chance, certainly not by intelligence, they took the direction it did not suit us to choose.

The Egyptian artillerymen had done good work in the cutting of timber during our absence. Splendid examples of the fine physique of the Egyptian fellahin, for a few extra piastres they were only too glad to slave at the work, getting through treble the amount that the sailors contributed. As they were paid according to the quantity which each individual brings in, an extraordinary stimulus was given to their exertions. Fine men that they are—and ours appeared to be of particularly good class—their heaviness contrasted strangely with the alert quickness of the slight savages on the banks, however lazy the latter in reality were. The complete nudity of the blacks naturally gives the better opportunity of appreciating the build of their figures, and in some cases of finely-formed men the modelling, proportion and outline of their figures, with one exception, are admirable. There is in these better examples a grace and cleanness in the chiselling, and a satisfying definition of the muscles under the skin ; as with the antelopes, fat enters not into suggestion, nor the horrid over-development which at present has vogue at home. The lines of chest and abdomen, though on the side of slightness, are perfect, and the marking of each series of muscles, and of the external divisions of the body, are distinctly yet delicately pronounced. The exception lies in the lower leg, which is invariably poor, in common with, perhaps, the majority of African blacks; and in general they fall short in one important particular, which produces inevitable disappointment, the whole system of build being detracted from by the spareness of the flesh-covering, resulting in an undeveloped and almost wasted appearance. Recollection wanders back to the great statue of David at Florence, to feel the greatest representation of power and beauty, and it is realized that the essential difference between the ancient statue and the living model before us lies, not merely in the better development of muscles and lower extremities, the shorter limbs, and the absence of coarseness in feet and hands, but in the nobility bestowed on mere outward form by the expression of mind, as well as of matter, which is evidenced in the great sculptor's marble.

Arrived once again at Kwoin, the fruit of our previous calls was immediately apparent. Not so many months before this visit the approach of a steamer was the signal for man, woman, and child, to bolt far out of reach. Now a small group of black figures awaited us on the bank by the grove of deleb palms. Belal and one Faragallah—distinct from the Dinka *bahari*—were our interpreters, being

Nuers who had been taken as slaves in their youth, and brought up as Arabs. But no education could restore to these men the front-teeth they had followed the fashion in losing, and it produced merely the slightest diffidence when it seemed better to descend from the glory of Egyptian clothing to the comparative indecency of a mere shoulder-cloth.

The two interpreters, being in charge of the business, evinced much excitement and sense of importance, issued instructions, and made lengthy and voluble explanations to their brothers on shore, which eventually led to a small ox being brought from the distant village. This was looked at disrespectfully, for the Nuers were careful in trading, and would not show their better goods first. Yet it was necessary to encourage them, and after much haggling and noise a price was agreed on in dhurra. Heaped on the shore were many sacks of this commodity, landed to demonstrate the *bona-fides* of our desire to trade. The completion of this transaction brought more cattle, and the people began to take courage and appear in greater numbers. After the men came the old, withered women, bringing their grass-woven baskets, plastered with cowdung to fill up interstices. Then would come the small boys, perhaps lugging an unwilling sheep or goat after them. It was difficult to persuade them that goats were not our object, for oxen were welcome to the exiles from civilization who laboured at clearing the "sudd" and welcomed fresh meat as conducive to health. It was essential as well that

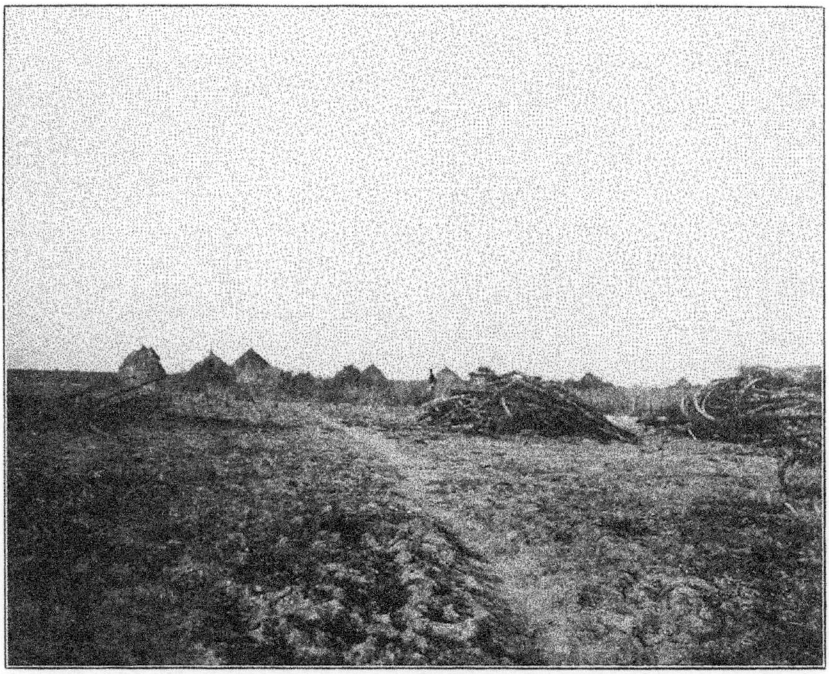

A NUER VILLAGE.

FARAGALLAH AND HIS LADY FRIENDS.

To face page 254.

the cattle should be in first-class condition, for I have remarked the extraordinary way they fall off in a small number of days when travelling on sandals up-river. So the lean and the halt were refused, and the villagers learnt that to bring poor ones was sheer waste of time.

I purposely mixed with the people, and exhausted a small stock of Arabic through the medium of Belal, who translated into Nuer, causing me to feel Arabic almost as my mother-tongue in comparison with the strange sounds, which seemed to defy analysis by the ear. Some approached nervously, gravely, with a gesture which seemed to signify disapproval or deprecation, but which in reality was a salaam; while others essayed conversation, which was best replied to by affirmative or non-committal grunts, which form an important feature in intercommunication!

A friendly attitude met generally with immediate response when once confidence had been established, and the exceptions to this in the Lower Zeraf were remarkably few, probably in no greater proportion, if so great, as would be met with amongst a similar crowd in England. One man brought his family in a canoe to assist, and refused to examine a mirror or stand for a photograph, either fearing the "evil eye," or to remain long in the vicinity of people who might prove, after all, to be false. Another sat on an ant-hill, twanging the native banjo, formed of five strings yielding consecutive notes in good tune, with a sour expression of face, yielding to no effort of friendliness. A third wandered aimlessly about, approaching repeatedly with the palms of his hands outstretched, and continually giving vent to some desire which even Belal failed to discover, and ended by saying "Magnun" (Mad).

Here the people were by no means so well fed as they were farther up-river, and showed correspondingly greater desire to trade, also explaining by signs in unmistakable manner that they were hungry, which of course is not necessarily worthy of credit! They were joined, as a last demonstration of belief in security, by unmarried maidens and the younger of the married women. The former often shuddered when they first saw their faces in a looking-glass—shuddered sometimes without too much reason—jumped out of their skins (which was all that they had to jump out of) when they saw a match struck, and felt passing rich with a handful of the white beads (*niaow*), which their feminine hearts craved for.

The looking-glass proved an immediate introduction to good-will, and its reputation evidently was bruited far and wide, for as days went on many came round, and it was obvious, from signs as they talked to the initiated, that it had been the subject of prior conversation. All the old scenes with the earlier visitors were faithfully re-enacted with later arrivals. Conceited "mere man" will be forgiven for saying that the truly remarkable fact was exhibited that the men showed themselves vastly vainer than women! Invariably the glass would at first be held close to the face, and on the reflection of an eye or nose being eventually discovered (which appeared as difficult as the focussing of a star through a telescope to the tyro), a loud shout of "Wah!" was sent up in surprise, sometimes fright. Reassured and instructed by companions, one would hold it at arm's length, and discover the whole of his remarkable features, and with a loud shout of "Gwah!" ("nice," "beautiful," "magnificent," was apparently the translation) he would dissolve into smiles of delight and self-admiration, having to be almost forcibly separated from his unlovely reflection, and returning time after time with repeated requests for further indulgence.

The "finder" of the camera, too, was an inexhaustible cause of amusement to men and maidens alike. The confidence shown by the latter in the *bona-fides* of the visitors was pleasing, and only the old crones would put in an instruction or caution, remembering days when fine words and good manners ended by their numbers being surrounded, and murder or slavery in exile resulting.

One day a middle-aged man approached me with a maid of barbarian beauty, and with solemnity made it apparent that he offered her me as a helpmate in life. Permitting him to continue his proposition, he explained, the shy beauty being quite acquiescent, that the consideration for his kindness would be thirty oxen (trade value in dhurra perhaps £15); the closed fists were thrust forward three times to indicate number. Cows would have been a welcome alternative to him, to the number of ten as equivalent, but they are almost impossible to obtain, so much store does the Nuer set by them. The lady was obviously exceedingly interested in what would be my decision, and doubtless had visions of riches in *niaow* and blue beads beyond dreams of avarice—clothing did not appeal to her; the paleness of my colour seemed by no means objectionable, and rotundness of figure in this land of the thin was a feature of beauty. Fortunately, matrimony being more a matter of business than of sentiment, I was enabled without great offence to decline, by means of a method of barter, as he would not come down to my figure, neither would I increase to his. Moreover, Belal was careful to explain that I was a peculiar person, and did not in the least appreciate the fair sex—in fact, I could only put up with one wife at home in my own country!

Though a matrimonial failure in the land of the Nuers, it did not deter another aspirant, and scruples as to respecting the feelings of the refused began to get blunted, especially as contemplation of their attractions caused one to sympathize with the feelings of James Brunton Stephens, the Queensland poet, who sang:

"Daughter of Eve, draw near; I would behold thee.
Good heavens! could ever arm of man enfold thee?
Did the same Nature that made Phryne mould thee?"

Apparently the marriage "ceremony" merely

consists of a feast on a slaughtered ox, and when married the girls immediately assume the palm-strip girdle, which is often made of string manufactured from the same finger-palm-leaf material.

The incredulity with which my monogamous peculiarity was received was consistent with the habits of the Nuers, who accumulate as large a collection of wives as their substitutes for pockets can afford. Naturally, when market value is so high, it is only the wealthy who get beyond two or three, while a Sheikh of importance will command a retinue of some fifty or sixty. As man is mortal and Sheikhs commonly well on in life, it is apparent that on the death of a Sheikh widows are liable to be thrown on the market in considerable numbers, and this fact was evidently, in the time of the ancient Nilotic lawgivers, recognized as a social problem necessary to be satisfied. So an expedient was hit upon for its solution, and Papa Nuer when lacking virility through extreme age, or lying sick unto death, appoints some one of his sons to act as husband to all his mothers but his own particular one, this coming into effect while Papa is *still alive.* What becomes of the unfortunate maternal parent who, in the nature of things, is left out in the cold does not appear, but, as the market is prevented from being overstocked, her case is no doubt easily absorbed. Now, Papa Shilluk is evidently not so far advanced in worldly wisdom as Papa Nuer, for he only ordains that the arrangement shall come into force after his death, and gets slyly knocked on the head, as a consequence, by some lusty young wife consumed with a desire to anticipate Nature.

Naturally, a Sheikh, possessing a greater number of wives (a doubtful advantage at his age), runs correspondingly greater risks, and the temptation to Papa Shilluk's wives to terminate the marriage contract by putting a period to the duration of his trials and troubles, thereby obtaining a healthy mate for themselves, must be considerable. It must be remembered that adultery on their part is punishable by a serious fine in cattle. All this cause of worry to an ailing man is avoided by the mental dexterity of Nuer lawgivers.

Strictly speaking, a widow does not marry again, and this gives rise to a custom which has a partial counterpart in the Old Testament. She certainly mates with a man, but she is not considered his wife, and her children by him are not credited to him in the family tree, but to the husband defunct. If with her new mate she prove barren, as proxy for her dead husband she " marries " some other girl, and enlists the assistance of her male friend to raise up seed to the dear departed. Thus it occurs that the child of a dead man and his widow may be flesh of neither of them, but by the means of procreation by deputies the continuance of the family name is assured. The system, if adopted in Europe, might prove popular with the representatives of old families who are " petering out."

On the death of a Nuer he will probably remain on the scene of his marital troubles and joys, for his burial-place is the inside of his hut, underground, or just outside his front-door. Utilitarianism prevails, and the proximity of the deceased does not appear to affect his late family, nor to interfere in the slightest with continued occupation of his house.

A Sheikh is in other ways by no means to be envied. He appears to be the recipient of great wealth from his visitors, but he will almost certainly be relieved of it by his subjects before he attains the sanctuary of his own hut, and it thus often happens that the man who receives the most ends up by having none. The son of the late Sheikh Diu, Woll Diu, who is physically a perfect example of manhood, had actually to be escorted by a bodyguard to his huts with the presents given by the Government, and the only imaginable parallel would be afforded by the spectacle of King Edward returning to Buckingham Palace laden with gifts from a foreign potentate, and running the gauntlet of an army of ravenous Socialists thirsting for the spoil.

This, if I recollect aright, occurred at a place called Louang Deng, which is a spot of considerable attraction, beautified by large-grown, thornless, shady, flowering trees. It is the joint Mecca of Dinkas and Nuers, who admit their common origin. It is very difficult to get particulars from the people as to their beliefs, but that given to my informant by the high-priest was to the effect that their ancestor, Deng Dit, had two sons, one of whom was the progenitor of the Nuer tribe, and the other of the Dinka. To the Dinka he presented a cow, and to the Nuer a cow-calf, or heifer. Not satisfied with his own portion, the Dinka coveted the property of the Nuer, even as Esau coveted that of Jacob. He stole his brother's cow-calf, and it was never restored. Therefore, pronounced Deng Dit, after persuasion and threat had failed, shall the Dinka henceforth and forever live by robbery, while the Nuer shall live by honourable war. And to this moment does this hold good, for even to-day the Government is occupied in arranging disputes between them, and in restoring to the Nuers cattle taken by stealth by the predatory Dinkas of the Khor Filus or of the south.

They also bear in awe more than in reverence a somewhat vague deity who is debited rather with maleficent powers than kindly intentions, this being a very common belief amongst all pagan races. Doubtless he is synonymous with the spirit of evil who took the form of the serpent in the Garden of Eden, and it is to be remarked that among various Sudanese tribes an evil spirit is believed to do ill to humanity by assuming the guise of a hyæna or other noxious beast harmful to man. In some cases it would appear that this spirit can be invoked for the service of some enemy of the victim, which belief is accountable for many subsequent imbroglios.

According to Belal, the Nuer country is divided into five provinces, namely, Jekang on the Sobat, Lau, Lak, Tiang, and Gaweir.

At Kwoin village, far up the river, I was overtaken by the Inspector, whose energy and enterprise was enormous and enviable. The pioneer work of the officials of these countries is done in the darkness of obscurity, and seldom becomes known to the world. Reports written from experience and knowledge are locked up or pigeon-holed at official headquarters, and it is too often left to the casual visitor, incompetent because time and opportunities are restricted, to chronicle imperfect records to the best of his ability.

An excuse to visit the village was afforded by the flight of duck in its direction, and it gave me an example in a small way of the difficulties of travel which the courageous pioneers, who undertake most enterprising journeys in their necessary exploratory work, undergo. Far in the evening haze the cattle could be seen streaming from their feeding-grounds on the bank of cracked clay, representing *terra firma* in this land still inchoate, and only half emerged from the protracted initial processes of creation. Fully a mile of morass intervened, and a couple of sturdy, amiable artillerymen were of welcome assistance in the first instance in negotiating the deeper patches of mud and water through which the track led. The lady who pushed a canoe through the winding, narrow waterway, and dragged it over the shallows, gave a profitable example of the more thorough method of progressing; repugnance at the black water was overcome, and the plunge taken. The bank eventually reached, on its borders were the few huts, quite irregularly placed, a little clean-swept space in front of the low door. Ancient Angelina sat, undisturbed by the coming of the stranger, gently rolling her gourd of beastly milk from side to side to make still more beastly butter. Near her is the smooth-sided hole in the ground wherein the corn is placed for crushing, for, in common with the Shilluks and Dinkas, the Nuers do not generally grind their corn as do the Arabs, but crush it laboriously with a heavy pestle some 6 feet long. Lack of concentration would appear to be a limitation of the Nuer in contrast to the Dinka, for Angelina would have to shout over a space of two or three hundred yards to the next few huts were she to see the robber Dinkas coming.

Here and there were deep holes of stagnant water, ideal breeding-places for mosquitoes and abominations, but still beloved of duck. Shrieks followed the report of my friend's twelve-bore, and amazement the fall of a mallard from a height by the mysterious power of the white man's magic; but recovery was quick on the object of our sport being seen in our hands, and a demand for *niaow* became observable as a feminine guide led us by the difficult track to our floating home.

CHAPTER XIII

"AHAI OW MAZADA!"

Our coming was awaited down-river at Kwoin with considerable interest. The news of our mission had spread far and wide, and there was a small party already assembled. As we neared them a snake caused a sensation on board. Probably caught up and whipped inboard by the stern wheel, it made for the deepest retreat it could find, and slid into the stokehole at one side while the stoker, who was fireman to Gordon, found it convenient to ascend just as expeditiously on the other. Owing to the heat, the infernal regions proved unpopular with the prototype of Satan, even as a temporary home, and, crossing the deck, it slithered away through the water, mid the curses of the crew, toward the bank where stood Adam and Eve.

Cattle rested under the deleb palms, whose golden, scented, but unfortunately stringy fruit was brought on board to us; dhurra was landed, and the well-worn process of bargaining was renewed, the price being generally four sacks of dhurra to the ox. A specially fine one would command five or six, but none were seen equal in quality to some which were taken from the Atwot Dinkas of the Mountain Nile during their recent rebellion.

There was now no shyness or hesitation on the part of the people; they came freely around, men, women, and children, the men entering the ghayassa, and on invitation even invading the lower deck of the steamer. Some of the women ventured exceedingly by visiting the sandal; their nervousness was extreme, and their precautions amusing. The men put their feet down, in taking a step, with the deliberation and care of a stork, but the ladies were cautious to an excess, fearing a fall. The gangway was level, and full 6 feet wide, and to the waders of marshes this would seem to be as secure as Westminster Bridge; but one would venture first, slowly, a foot at a time, balancing with bent body and legs, holding the hand of her sister behind, gingerly treading every inch of the *sigala*, and expressing unbounded relief at the safe termination of the hazardous journey. Yet the same women would entrust themselves without a qualm to the tender mercies of an unstable canoe with brittle clay ends!

To my mind, the people generally evinced much more intelligence than many of the raw natives I came across in Mashonaland in 1895. I then had great difficulty, when short of food, in explaining that I wanted eggs; various graphical illustrations proving resultless, a pencil outline was fruitlessly resorted to, then shaded in, proving uproariously successful only when a crack was delineated, with the head and neck of a chicken emerging. The Nuers understand a sketch more quickly, naming a lion from a very unworthy drawing, and explaining that lions, though very numerous, did not trouble them much, as if let alone by man they would generally reciprocate such neglect. I gathered that their word for "lion" had a strange similarity to the English, approximating the sound of *aleean*, the accent on the second syllable, with the first very short. The Arabic word for "woman" is *mara*, *mariam* also being used—a fairly obvious derivation of the name "Mary." The difficulties of interpretation led to uncertainty of the Nuer equivalent, which sounded like *man*, but of this I could not get confirmation.

The expressions for "father" and "mother" appear to be root words which have come down from remote ages through the multitudinous branches of the human race. The Dinka and Lur for "mother" is *ma*, the Sandeh *na*, and the Bari *mama;* while for "father" the Sandeh say *ba*, the Bari and Bamba *baba*, and the Mombottu *papanque*. The Bari go a step farther with the word "sister," and say *sasser*. Probably Cain used the same terms.

The names of Nuers are generally monosyllabic, but, as in England, they as a rule rejoice in two. A Chinese gravestone in Adelaide, Australia, recorded the sepulture of a man appropriately or otherwise named "Gong Up." Here we come across such names as Toi Thif, Uz Kir, Bied Uz, or Bai Gam. They at least have the merit of simplicity.

One very tall man put in an appearance here, and I greatly desired to measure him, but to this he entertained the strongest objection. Some superstitious folk in England have an aversion to the height of their children being taken, connecting it with the undertaker's requirements in regard to a coffin; but such an idea formed no reason here, as such luxuries are not indulged in. A ruse became necessary, and by stealth a seven-foot spear was placed beside him, over which, a giant amongst tall men, he still towered by fully 6 inches.

Another fine fellow, almost approaching this Nuer in height, appeared with a terrible hole in his face, the upper jaw-front being missing, and the nasal orifices being one with the mouth. His upper teeth were displaced, and protruded at all angles. This was occasioned by the attack of an elephant, which, throwing him down, had thrust his tusk into the poor fellow's face, causing a wound which would have destroyed anyone but a savage. I endeavoured to get details from him of the accident, but he evinced the greatest aversion to being questioned on what was apparently a highly distasteful subject.

The explanation of the sleek, comparatively cleanly looks of the women, who merely show the marks on their knees and shins caused by kneeling on moist earth in the course of their daily work, is due to their abstention from the habit of painting themselves white, to their practice of shaving their heads entirely, and to the fact that, unlike the cattle-herding men, they do not sleep on burnt-ash beds, but in their own huts. One of the quaint sights of the country is to see an ash-covered, lead-coloured Nuer after walking up to his middle in water. His head is also caked in adhesive masses of ash mixture, his face, and chest to his middle are of the whitey-grey of a horrid corpse, while below the waist he is a beautiful, glistening black! It is to be hoped that the effect of the hair pomade is at least disinfectant, and that the absence of hair on the body of both sexes conduces to freedom from some classes of parasites.

Small boys crowded round one, laughing and joking; young men and old warriors joined in investigations, never the sign of a liberty being taken; and long conversations, with much emphasis and gesticulation, were alternated with expressions of friendliness and horrible smiles. Time after time, toward the end of my visit, a lanky fellow would approach, with a well-meaning grin all over his face, and from the heights far above me would bend and shout down in my face, " Ahai ow mazada!" It sounded uncommonly like the word " murder," as the consonants were but slightly pronounced; but his evident pleasure gave the lie to such a deduction. Learning that the meaning was an expression of content with my personality, I tried its effect, on my return to Fashoda, on a solitary Nuer who had been brought into hospital, and who, separated from his companions, speaking no Arabic, and desperately lonely, burst into wreaths of smiles when I shouted "Murder!" into his face!

A dance of small boys was voluntarily arranged by the Nuers for my entertainment. Led by a mature instructor, who faced them, they had the advantage of a stringed band in true civilized fashion. Certainly, it was confined to one instrument, a gourd banjo, and had but the usual five notes; still, it was played in tune and in time, with a drum accompaniment struck by the finger on the sounding-board, but with no vestige of an air. Primitive as ever, the dance was undoubtedly erotic, and, though comparatively mild in character, it appeared a combination of the *danse du ventre* and the Maori *haka*.

Many of the men wore the ivory armlets which are such characteristic ornaments of these Nilotic negroids. Worked out of the upper and hollow portions of the elephant's tusk, they are shaped in different outlines, the sections of some showing considerable taste in the design. Some are cross-sections of the tusk, others cut longitudinally; and such is the slightness of bone in these people, that ladies in Europe, on endeavouring to pass them over the elbow, marvel to think it to be possible by a full-grown man. Some of the finer specimens are said to be heirlooms, and it seemed perhaps sinful to bargain for them. However, the Nuers preferred the three skeins of blue beads which I offered them in exchange, deeming themselves much the gainers, and all parties were satisfied.

My partiality for these curiosities having become known—those common, ordinary, everyday things which the foolish white man gives beautiful blue beads for—a youngster thrust under my notice an inferior, exceedingly old one, having little but its peculiar shape to recommend it to me. I waved it away, not requiring it; but the youth was so anxious, that out of sheer kindness of heart I put my hand in my pocket and gave him an empty brass cartridge-case from my shot-gun, of far less intrinsic value than that valuable object of barter, an empty ·303 case. The transaction had been watched with breathless interest, and a shout of derision went up on the completion of the bargain. The black bystanders roared at the fool—yes, but *I* was the fool! I had been "done brown" by a bit of a boy, who had palmed off on me, in exchange for very valuable consideration, a piece of most miserable rubbish!

It was apparent that a very large proportion of the people had never before set eyes on a white man. The nearest approach to any kind of familiarity—and then it was not intended as such—was when one would touch my unbuttoned shirt in order to come to some sort of conclusion as to whether or not I were white all over. The fact that my collar-bones did not jut out like the hip-bones of a starved ox, as did theirs, seemed to excite admiration and envy.

The terror of one dear old lady when she set eyes on me first is for ever unforgettable. For seventy years this wrinkled and wasted old thing must have lived amongst ordinarily coloured skins, and now was fated to confront the ghastly sight which a white face presented. Mere anæmia in no way came near it; the corpse-like hue of her ash-coloured sons paled—I should say darkened—beside it. Sick with horror, she clasped her head in both hands, turned away with wild shrieks, and covered her face, which to me was a matter of considerable comfort, it not being beautiful.

It was interesting, too, to try the effect of foods on their uncultivated tastes. Great curiosity was evinced as to my methods of eating, and small crowds stood by on the shore, remarking on the strange methods in use by the white man on board. Sugar was an abomination to them, save after a while to the usual small boy. The puff biscuits, of which there are too many in Huntley and Palmer's "mixed" tins, were tasted gingerly, and then thrown away. These are particularly useful in the Sudan for the purpose of creating a thirst when the heat is insufficient, and I perfectly appreciated the action of these Nuers when, in their endeavour to lubricate their desiccated throats, the poor victims proceeded to lower the level of the river. Fish rissoles received but scant appreciation, perhaps also because they were fresh and not high in flavour!

After all, milk is good, when one has conquered one's scruples; and, again, dhurra as bread—dhurra boiled with grease, whole in grain or as flour—dhurra as merissa—dhurra as um-bil-bil or the Nuer equivalent—dhurra in fermented flakes with water: what a marvellous variety of food, and what need of greater?

They rarely eat their cattle, unless the latter die, which is reminiscent of a way some have in England of killing a beast on the point of death, so that it may be sent to market with a clear conscience. One case recurs to me in which an animal so treated was discovered to have been suffering from anthrax unrecognized by the farmer, and only escaped the market by the vigilance of an official. Tobacco is cultivated, and their large pipes resemble those of the Dinka and Shilluk.

On going ashore the last day I was soon made aware of something unusual. Two moments after approaching a group I was surprised to see all the women and girls, some thirty or forty in number, running away in a bunch. As this left only the men of the party, not understanding the manœuvre, I got within reach of the boat, but was soon reassured.

They followed a tall man, new as a visitor, who held a cylindrical object over his head, and uttered sharp guttural commands in harsh tones to his following. Then, all facing me about fifty paces away, they sang a weird song, and advanced, still singing, toward me, the old Sheikh-priest, for such he appeared, intermingling his rough voice with the not quite unmelodious tones of the women.

Four yards away they all stopped, and crouched, or knelt, on their knees, and then came a performance for all the world like the responses in our English Church service. With wonderful vigour and emphasis the Sheikh, Buz Nyal by name, recited a short sentence jolted out in a tone so severe that he might be intending to devour the maids. His congregation replied with a somewhat more lengthy response, and, just as happens in church, slightly before the end of their sentence Parson Buz Nyal had begun his next invocation. It was for all the world like, "We beseech Thee to hear us, good Lord." I found it impossible to avoid a comparison with the situation at home, where the clergyman holds a somewhat similar sway over the feminine mind. Here on the part of his subjects was an obedience amounting to as near adoration as is possible to the undeveloped native mind, and on the Sheikh's part a masterful domination—influence is too weak a word—which was meekly submitted to.

Buz Nyal wore the spiked rings and bracelets with which the Nuers lacerate disobedient wives' backs (of the latter there seemed to be plenty); his nails were exceedingly long, as are those of the Chinese; his hair long and fuzzy, growing as though he were running full speed and leaving it behind in the wind, only being retained in position by the bond of a cowrie circlet.

Here is a land where our suffragette friends might well indulge their energies, and perhaps achieve actual martyrdom in a protest against the use of Adam's dreadful jewellery.

At this moment, the responses ended, not knowing the degree of importance of the good Buz Nyal, but judging the time had come when he expected a present, and having nothing else handy, I placed a supply of white beads, known as *niaow*, in his hands. Baker recounts the mistake of pet ostriches in camp at Khartoum, who devoured these beads with alacrity under the false impression that they were dhurra. Buz Nyal's palsied hand could hardly retain them, and as a gift being obviously insufficient, the services of Belal, the interpreter, were called in. Fortunate it was for me that I did so, as the event proved. A vast talk was indulged in by Buz, mainly consisting of a recital of the importance and value of the presents made to other chiefs by the Government. Eventually, after lengthy discussion, a cloth sufficient to cover the trunk of the body when tied at two opposite corners and slung over the shoulder, half a dozen coils of brass wire, a string of large black beads spotted with white (*gianator*), and a couple of skeins of the blue ones, proved satisfactory, with a sack of the dhurra thrown in.

" Halass " (Finished) was cried, formal friendship was declared, and holding Belal's hand, palm upwards, before him, Buz Nyal spat into it as a seal to an unwritten document.

Shortly afterwards he had a very determined and emphasized conversation with me—he was nothing if not emphatic—his words being interpreted as an expression of pleasure at seeing me, or the Nuer equivalent, and ending in the gift of a further small handful of beads. Then came an exhibition of kinship with Solomon. In accordance with the prerogative of a Sheikh previously described, two women came up and begged him for beads. Competition was keen, and words became high, angering Buz Nyal; so he took the bull by the horns, and ended the dispute by pitching the beads far into the grass, scattering them beyond reclamation. His mood suddenly changed, and, turning to me with a smile, in modulated tones he expressed his hope—as Belal translated—that he had not made me angry, and that I did not think that he undervalued my gift, assuring me that it was necessary to end the dispute in the drastic manner I had witnessed.

Another instance of unexpected politeness was afforded when an old gentleman, clad in a shoulder-cloth ragged and discoloured with age, approached me with many gentle signs, and begged me to sit down in front of him; pointing out the existence of a very obvious rent, he made the sign of a needle and thread, by which one would gather that he had previously come into contact with civilization. Seeing also his dissatisfaction with the

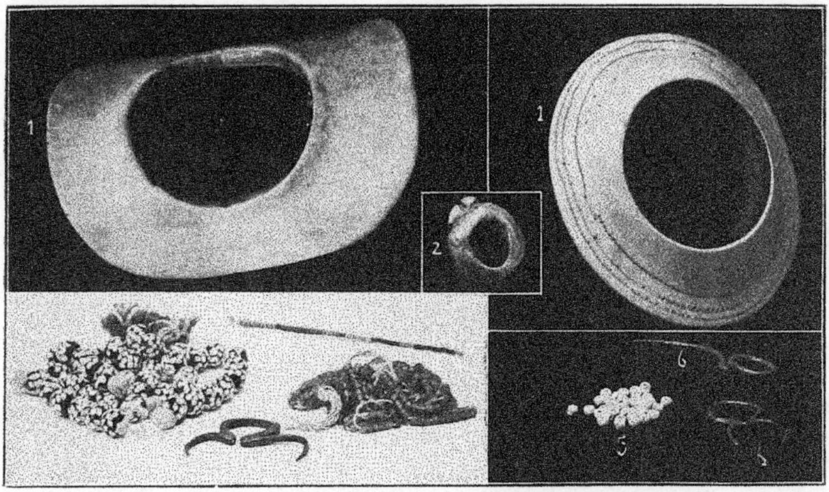

IVORY ARMLETS AND NUER CURRENCY.

1, Ivory armlets ; 2, ivory ring ; 3, *gianator* beads ; 4, blue beads ; 5, *maow ;* 6, iron and brass rings ; 7, woman's lip ornament.

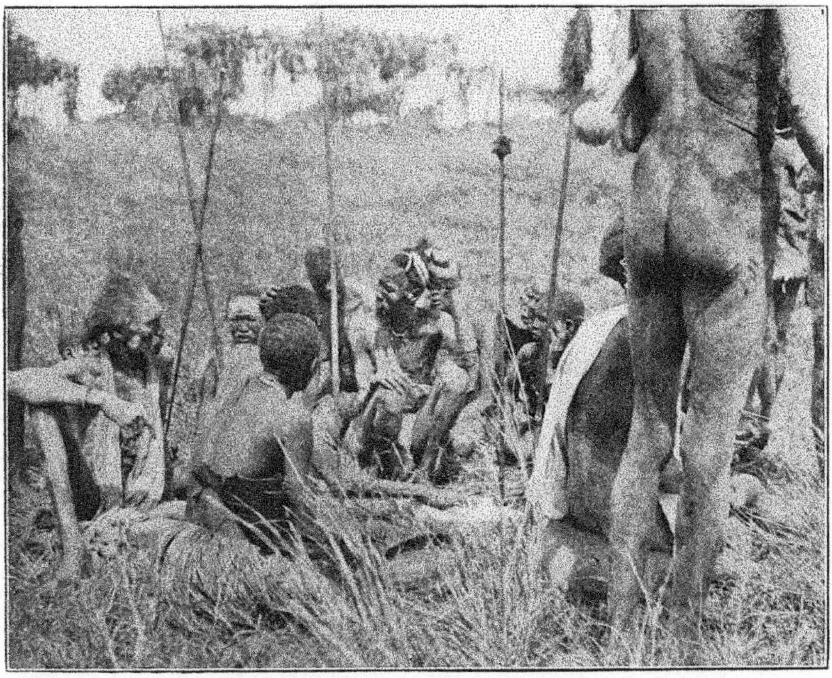

BUZ NYAL DISCUSSES THE PRESENTS.

To face page 276.

frayed, unsewn edge of his cloth, I turned it up and roughly hemmed it, his face a picture of pleasure. His words at the finish were numerous and politely intoned, a patent expression of gratitude quite unlooked for in natives, and later I was further surprised to see him interviewing Belal, who explained that my friend was anxious to know if I would stay till next day, as he desired to give me a backsheesh. My delight at the outlook was modified by uncertainty as to whether it would have taken the form of a daughter or sheep!

This all demonstrates the existence of a basis which could be improved upon, a fact which would give one pleasure but for the fears that enlightenment may bring other evils in its train to replace or add to the indigenous ones. The intellect certainly is there, else why should Belal and Faragallah, brought up as slaves to the Arab, show such superiority?—an advantage they certainly feel, looking down on their uninitiated brethren with the finest contempt.

A further sack of dhurra was vouchsafed to Buz Nyal, half of which he placed on the ground on a spot hardened by water being poured over it, then assembling a dozen of the poorer women of the village, unbecomingly on hands and knees, in a circle round the heap. All was still—the strained, intense quiet of the start of the hurdle race—until Buz gave the word. Then were the forces of Nature let loose in a marvellous scramble for the small, roundish grains. Hunger and avarice impelled the poor hags, and their speed and agility soon cleared the ground of every trace of a grain, the very dust being raked up and sifted, that none should be lost.

Then came the finish of the cattle-purchase. Buz Nyal, having failed to extract another sack of dhurra from me, had a final conversation with us through Belal, clinching matters by spitting once more into Belal's hand and then deluging that unfortunate's face. Belal blinked involuntarily during the operation, but stood it bravely, being to the manner born. Happy was I that I had brought him as deputy. Buz Nyal ended up by asking in turn for my eyeglasses, mirror, and spy-glass, and refusal by no means offended him.

I noted on the bank a heap of briquette coal, which had been there prior to our first visit, and, on expressing surprise that it was left quite unguarded, I was assured that it would be perfectly safe to leave one's goods and chattels unattended amongst the people—they would not be interfered with. Dishonesty would appear to attend the march of civilization, for so admirable a trait does not endure long.

I had been overtaken here by the Inspector, who had been up an out-of-the-way *khor*, Nwaznyel, for the purpose of visiting villages, and tumbled into luck on the way. As he passed by a game-track through a region of grass, he was faced, at about 50 yards, by a bull buffalo, which a clean shot through the brain instantly dropped. Great was the joy of the Nuers, who aided in cutting it up and disposed of most of its meat; and the servants having gone back to the steamer, carrying some of the meat and the skull, he tried to persuade the Sheikh to accompany him also. Great was his disagreeable surprise to see the effect of this kind proposition; for the Nuer immediately started to waltz round him, jabbing his spear in a war-dance and in dangerous proximity. No amount of quiet expostulation had any effect, and it became very nearly a question as to whether it might not be necessary, in sheer self-defence, to shoot the raging black devil. He was left to his antics, and, on explanation being asked, it appeared the poor fellow was mad, and had got it into his head that the Government of the Madhi had returned, and that my friend's invitation was merely a ruse to decoy him on to the boat and enslave him. It is an illustration of how the horrid fear exists still, and one may marvel, indeed, not at the suspicion and shyness, but at the degree of readiness to respond to any kind of overture.

As our boat slowly drifted away from the shore, our dark friends made a last celebration of our short visit. The young men with the clubs and long spears rushed down the bank in a war-dance, crouching and darting alternately forward. Maidens stood with their arms round each other, and a crowd lined the river to bid us good-bye.

The journey downstream in my friend's boat was

characterized by small incident, and the sailors on my own floating home had the best of it as they followed a few hours later, marking a lion *en route.*

A fair, white-eared cob was bagged on one bank; the wood on the other grew dense, and great herds of tiang and waterbuck grazed on the spaces between. Some fine heads appearing amongst them, I landed to stalk—a proceeding vastly more difficult where there are numbers of animals rather than few, as the coveted head is usually in a spot beyond the position of others who have to be passed. They moved slowly on as some saw me, covering fully a mile ere they stopped. A low stretch of bush favoured, and now, far from the river, the opportunity came. I fired, and, hitting low, broke the front-leg of the buck, which moved off. Lying quiet—for I thought myself still unperceived—I awaited events, and was right; for he soon stopped again, and a second shot then brought him down. Hanging a piece of white paper on a bush, I returned to the steamer, and found the men, replete with buffalo and cob meat, unwilling to trouble to fetch the head in, the walk being long in the depth of the forest. To my surprise, I perceived, on getting back, that the crows had already been at work, having picked out the eyes of the buck.

The days of shooting were now coming to an end, and the most had to be made of remaining opportunity in a country still replete with game. Early in the morning I saw specks against the bush belt, which the glass resolved into ostriches, and a large herd of tiang, that ungainly animal resembling a cross between roan antelope and hartebeest. For three mortal hours, with a stove-hot south wind blowing, I stalked those wary tiang over eight or ten miles of rough country with scarcely any cover, never getting within 400 yards. Deeply disgusted and blaming myself, I rejoined my companion and tested my shooting on a solitary tiang. I was now too exhausted to properly stalk. At 350 yards a bullet passed between his legs, striking the ground behind him ; at 400 yards the same thing occurred ; so the chances of fate were against me.

But in the afternoon, on our debouching into the White Nile, came the last opportunity to kill "Mrs. Gray." This sounds murderous indeed, but the crime was most tempting. She—or, to be accurate, he—was visible on the dry land, the white patch over the shoulders showing bright in the distance against the dark body.

The difficulty which presented itself was how to land. First came tall grass floating on the water—the steamer ploughed through that ; then grass growing in two-feet-deep water—two planks assisted me there for a few steps ; then I sank to my knees in water and grass-roots, which endowed me with courage, and so I plunged onward. A section of nearly dry land ensued, and I thought that my troubles were over, for a few yards ahead the grass was to all appearances burnt black and dry to the ground. So on went my scout Faragallah, his legs being longer than mine by some feet, and soon I discerned him in difficulties. "Moya ketir" (Much water), called he; but "Mrs. Gray" was on the opposite side, and I boldly started into the morass. It was not merely a bed of mud and superincumbent water, but a network through its depths and above them of tangled cane-reeds in all stages of burntness and rot. The caked black mass on the surface at first had been hardened by the sun's rays, and the feet sank but a few inches into the entanglement. Then a step or two forward, and my foot smashed through the crust; one leg broke down into 4 feet of foul black water and rottenness, and I found myself sprawling on all fours in the filth, now a little more supported through the less concentrated distribution of weight. The trouble now was how to extricate one hand or one foot and place it before the other, and I thought of the remarkably ludicrous sight I must present to the binoculars on the steamer, though, as a matter of fact, the good men were somewhat concerned at my plight.

I felt my Ross monocular go under water, and nearly lost my spectacles, in the course of the struggle; while, as I extricated one hand to advance it a foot, the other sank deeper, and, depressing my head to the surface, checked further movement. The grass swarmed with a huge variety of red ant, which made ferocious attacks, and horrid beasties of various descriptions installed themselves on my skin. How any progress was made is now incomprehensible, and my mind is a blank; but struggling and floating, and pushing and wading, recklessly throwing myself forward, clutching what stalks remained above water and pushing them under me, I fought through the fifty odd yards now intervening between me and dry land, and the 'cute "Mrs. Gray." The last 10 yards were the worst of the lot; I sank up to my neck, and went almost under, my servant afterwards laughingly bringing the mirror for me to see the black bits of grass on my teeth.

Then I threw myself on the ground while the water coursed out of pockets and breeches, and the boots sang a squeaky song as my feet slipped about in the water they retained. "Malesh" (Never mind); I moved on, while "Mrs. Gray" laughed to see such sport and moved on as well. And so she played her game; taking precaution to move where the grass was shortest, she kept me in sight for want of cover, and less than 400 yards never separated us. So, after spending much time, thought, and malediction, in devising impossible methods, I came to the conclusion that the superlative sport of "Mrs. Gray" in this region consisted in witnessing bipeds exhaust themselves in the depths of the evil marsh, then in turn to exhaust their patience by keeping just carefully out of possible range. It really must possess a ludicrous side and be rather fun.

So "Mrs. Gray" became not my victim, and I searched for a spot where I might approach the river without again undergoing so trying an experience. It was found in a Shilluk *meshra* farther downstream, a tiny track through the green, unburnt grass, leading deeper and deeper into the water. It appeared as though I should have to brave the crocodiles, and swim to the steamer, which could not approach very near, when my eye caught sight of the ambatch raft of a Shilluk, half hidden in the grass. This consists of a number of half-rotten sticks of the light, pithy wood, thick at the base and tapering off quickly, thus lending itself well to being tied into a raft with taper bows and a square stern. Joy filled my breast; squatting on it, finding myself seated in water as the raft sank beneath me, with a push from the sailors behind I paddled my way to the steamer, an object indeed. As I left there was an ominous rustle in the reeds, the sailors cried "Timsagh" (Crocodile), and scattered like fluff on the breeze.

Later on, in the darkness, came shouts from the bank of the river, and a noise as if of penny trumpets. This probably indicated a fight going on, which is not of infrequent occurrence just here, though gratitude for mercies vouchsafed should move the inhabitants, inasmuch as in four years their cattle possessions increased by no less than sixty-six per cent.

The Garden of Eden left behind—its serpent slid down a tree as I approached it one morning, and entered the river—its inhabitants were left to the

A FAVOURITE ATTITUDE.

"GOOD-BYE."

To face page 284.

good influences of firmness and sympathy exhibited so nobly by its Governor.

Kodok slid back into the past, and Renk gave memories of the long camel ride from the Dinder. Goz Abu Guma, by Hillet Abbas, was passed close by the island of Abba, where the Mahdi spent the early days of his religious development, and where, inland and opposite, is Um Debreikat, the field which witnessed the crushing of his movement through the death of the Khalifa and his remnant of army.

Here the dhurra-birds came in their millions, wee creatures that had appeared on the Dinder in places, and produced an astounding effect at close quarters. In the distance there is a black cloud of smoke, rapidly moving; it advances, extends, changes direction and form in bewildering fashion, increases and pales in its colour, condenses and thickens, twisting and twirling at speed with all the strange movements of a skirt-dancer's robe. The birds will descend on a plantation of dhurra with all the destructiveness of the locust pest, stripping the plants of their grain in incredible time, with ruin to those who depend on it.

Dueim, on the western bank, was passed by, where the Governor's pier consisted of two old whisky cases, a sunken canoe, bottom up, a telegraph-pole, and an angarib, and where caravans of camels brought gum from Kordofan.

Swiftly the boat glided down the stream till Gordon's tree stood out on the eastern bank, marking the spot of his anxious vigils; then the Blue Nile challenged the White for room for its waters which have rolled past Khartoum, and the end came at last with the discharge of ivory and an elephant's ear which some Arab had brought down to mud Omdurman.

Here lived the hero of the following story given me by my friend on the Zeraf, who when resident in Omdurman possessed a young lion, which was extraordinarily tractable, and entertained great respect from his youth upwards for the fist of his master. As he grew larger the respect still remained, but foundation for it diminished to vanishing-point. As a youngster the blow used to hurt, and Leo would put back his ears, shut his eyes, and brace his nerves for the shock. Not realizing that the strength of his master did not increase proportionately with his own growth, he was as scared of the fist when three-quarters grown as he was when a baby. He had a playful habit of waiting behind doors, or, on a person walking along the verandah, unsuspecting his play, would jump out on him merely in fun, evincing keen disapproval if his intention were balked.

Lions are supposed not to climb, but if the grave story related, not on the China seas, but on the broad Nile, will hold water, my last resource when I see a lion evaporates. Leo learned to climb, and one day when he had scratched up a telegraph-pole, and rested his chin on the top, he suddenly caught sight of his master. Panic seized him at the idea of results following interference with Government property, and at the thought of the fist, losing his presence of mind, he missed grip and slid with his legs grasping the pole, and an expression of agony on his face, from the top to the bottom, landing on his tail with a terrible bump. He was sorry for himself for a long time after, but as a deputation of influential inhabitants of Omdurman came to protest against his continued residence at large, and threatened an evacuation of the city by its 40,000 inhabitants as an alternative, he had to console himself, and recover under unwelcome restraint.

Returned to the centre of government, a glance back may not come amiss. The Sudan covers a vast area, and presents a remarkable diversity of problems, differing with the various conditions of the provinces.

Dongola is rich, and as settled as a province of Lower Egypt; Khartoum has the unique characteristic of being the old centre of Mahdism, with a neighbouring city of Arabs mainly hostile at heart, regretful of the old slave days and their enormous percentage of profit; it is a country where thousands of sheep and goats can be seen watering at the river.

There is the Blue Nile province, rich in possibilities when irrigation is taken in hand, and where Mahdism has since recrudesced; and that of Sennaar, once with its Abyssinian question, and highly advanced in actual rather than relative progress, having had the advantage of particularly practical and intelligent administration: the Arabs' productive powers have been encouraged with success, and the home of an old civilization is being revived after the desolation and depopulation of the past thirty years.

Then comes the Upper Nile province, where the problem is vastly different, being one of instructing the negroid element from the beginning, rather than the semi-cultivated Arab; a gaining of the confidence of native barbarians, and the mastery of their laws and customs; ruling through native laws where possible, and—what is new—enforcing the judgments. Moreover, the endeavour is made to insure intertribal peace among a turbulent people, to relieve districts stricken with famine by means full of wisdom, to educate gradually peoples who as yet are little beyond the level of animals.

In the Mongalla province, until recently part of the Upper Nile province, there is the "Lado Enclave" and the Congo Free State adjoining, requiring judgment and tact, unexplored and barbarian regions to the east, and the broken-down remnants of the great Bari race to revive.

Westward is the Bahr-el-Ghazal, with its enormous difficulties in unhealthy climate and superfluity of swamps, bounded by the great forests of the Congo, and with great possibilities in rubber and timber.

Kordofan, with its combination of much trade in the north, and warlike races in the *gebels* of the south, the centre where the slave trade dies hardest, adjoins the province of Darfur, which has relapsed into native conditions of rule since Gessi fled from revolt, and is governed by a nominal tributary until railways develop and communication is rendered more easy, which is now within sight.

Every year sees progress, and the extension of the railway over the Blue Nile and up to Sennaar, with the bridging of the White at Hillet Abbas for the tapping of Kordofan, tightens the grip of the white man for the welfare of the country. I have seen something of the work done by the Governors and Inspectors of various provinces, and can speak in nothing but terms of admiration of the whole-hearted devotion to the highest and best interests of their charges. There is no mere perfunctory discharge of administrative duties, but a forceful, intelligent, personal mastery of every condition and each individual problem, a painstaking grasp of detail, a masterful grip where the master is needed. One is impressed by the intense personal interest that is displayed, and the amount of hard work voluntarily undertaken in a climate where no man passes long unscathed, under conditions of life which are at the best difficult, and often entail great hardship and exhausting exertion, both mental and physical.

Khartoum, with all its varied responsibilities for the general conduct of the country as a whole, with its social constellation, its pleasant residences, garden-surrounded, and its touch with the exterior world, has much to be grateful for in having the services of men who courageously bear the burden and heat of the day in the wilds, many of whom have for years lived in grass huts, travelled vast distances, often carrying their lives in their hands, and have grappled with difficulties conquered and disposed of long before reaching the ears of the central officials.

Khartoum and the Sudan generally were placed on broad and sound lines by Lord Kitchener, and some of the men in responsible positions are even yet those who went through the arduous work of the war. With these the working out of Kitchener's lines in their detail has rested in the past, and who can say they have failed in their demonstration of the quality of the work which, of all nations, it is ordained that Great Britain shall do?

That those who are following on may be imbued with the same methods of thoroughness, and will show the same self-sacrificing earnestness and practical intelligence which have characterized the pioneers of administration here, will be the securest guarantee for a successful solution of the undoubtedly serious problems which confront the rulers of this heterogeneous population and difficult land.

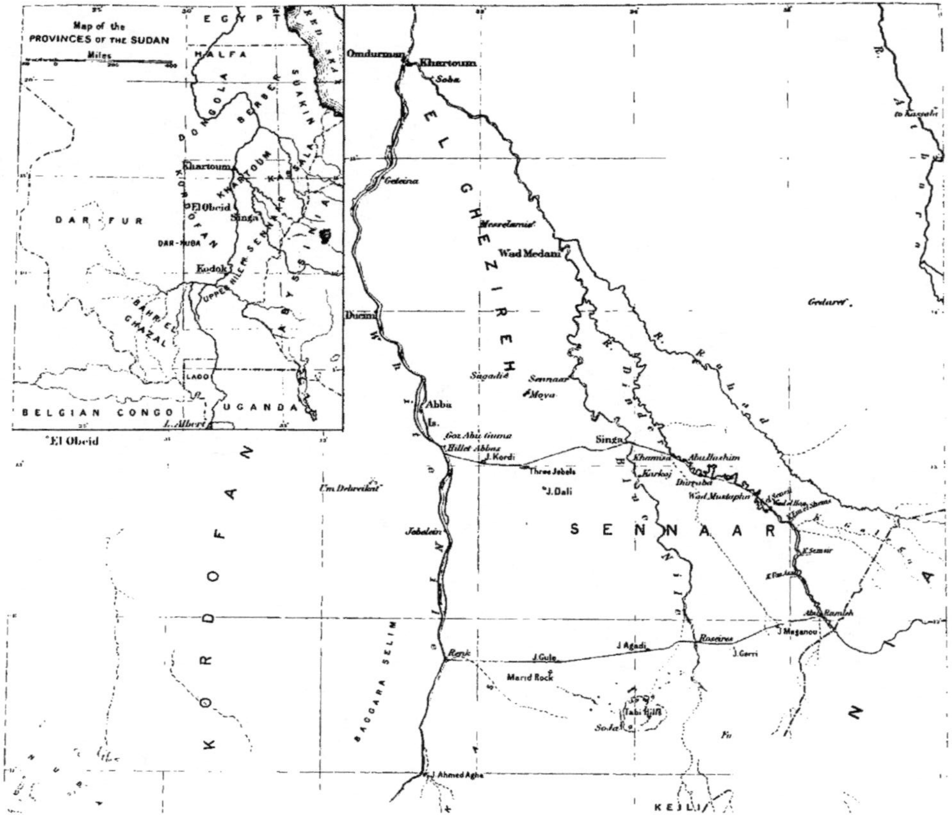

Map of the
PROVINCES OF THE SUDAN
Miles
EGYPT
RED SEA
HALFA
DONGOLA
BERBER
SUAKIN
KHARTOUM
KASSALA
Khartoum
El Obeid
Singa
SENNAAR
DAR-FUR
DAR-NUBA
KORDOFAN
Kodok
UPPER NILE
ABYSSINIA
BAHR EL GHAZAL
LADO
UGANDA
BELGIAN CONGO
L. Albert
El Obeid
Omdurman
Khartoum
Soba
Geteina
EL GHEZIREH
Mesalamia
Wad Medani
Duem
Sagadie
Sennaar
Moya
Abba Is.
Goz Abu Guma
Hillet Abbas
J. Kordi
Three Jebels
J. Dali
Um Dehreiket
Singa
Khamisa
Karkoj
Abu Hashim
Wad Mustapha
SENNAAR
Jebelein
BAGGARA SELIM
Renk
J. Gule
Marid Rock
J. Agadi
Roseires
J. Gerri
J. Meganou
Abu Ramleh
Tabi Hills
Soda
J. Ahmed Agha
KORDOFAN
R. Dinder
R. Rahad
R. Atbara
to Kassala
Gedaref
KEJLI

INDEX

B.

C.

BILLING AND SONS, LTD., PRINTERS, GUILDFORD

* 9 7 8 1 3 3 2 0 1 8 2 8 4 *

WS - #0024 - 230523 - C0 - 229/152/20 - PB - 9781332018284 - Gloss Lamination